# THE MARTYRS OF INDIA

DIVYANSH RAZDAN

Made with ❤ on the Notion Press Platform
www.notionpress.com

*This book is dedicated to all those freedom fighters who fought with British and successfully liberated our motherland India. Many of us know them and many do not. If you want to know more about some freedom fighters of India, yo have come to the right knowing the history of our own country is must especially about the people who sacrificed their lives to free India. Have a happy and enjoyable reading.*
*Thank You.*

# Contents


*Prologue* · vii

1. SUBHAS CHANDRA BOSE · 1
2. BHAGAT SINGH · 26
3. CHANDRA SHEKHAR AZAD · 46
4. KHUDIRAM BOSE · 53
5. SARDAR VALLABHBHAI PATEL · 66
6. MANGAL PANDEY · 103
7. BAL GANGADHAR TILAK · 109
8. VINAYAK SAVARKAR · 125
9. NATHURAM GODSE · 142
10. RANI LAKSHMI BAI · 148
11. UDHAM SINGH · 157
12. LALA LAJPAT RAI · 164
13. MADAN MOHAN MALVIYA · 172

# Prologue

**Current Map of India (Bharat)**

# CHAPTER ONE

# SUBHAS CHANDRA BOSE

**Summary:**

*Subhas Chandra Bose was an Indian nationalist whose defiance of British authority in India made him a hero among many Indians, but his wartime alliances with Nazi Germany and Imperial Japan left a legacy vexed by authoritanism, anti-semitism and military failure. The honorific 'Netaji' ("Respected Leader") was first applied to Bose in Germany in early 1942- by the Indian soldiers of the Indische Legion and by the German and Indian officials in the Special Bureau for India in Berlin. It now used throughout India.*

Subhash Chandra Bose

## 1897-1921 : Early Life

*Subhas Chandra Bose was born to Bengali parents Prabhavati Bose and Janakinath Bose on 23 January 1897 in Cuttack, Odisha in India, but was then part of the Bengal Presidency in British India. Prabhavati had her first child at age 14 and 13 children thereafter. Subhas was the ninth child and sixth son. Janakinath, a successful lawyer and government pleader, was loyal to the government of British India and scrupulous about matters of language and the law. A self-made man from the rural outskirts of Calcutta, he had remained in touch with his roots, returning annually to his village during the Pooja holidays. Eager to join his five school-going older brothers, Subhas entered the 'Baptist Mission's Protestant European School' in Cuttack in January 1902. English was the medium of all instruction in the school, the majority of the students being European or Anglo-Indians of mixed British and India ancestry. The curriculum included English-correctly written and spoken-Latin, the Bible, good manners, British geography and British history; no Indian languages were taught. The choice of the school was Janakinath's, who wanted his sons to speak flawless English with flawles intonation, believing both to be important for access to the British in India. The school contrasted with Subhas's home, where only Bengali was spoken. At home, his mother worshipped the Hindu Goddesses Durga and Kali, told stories from the epic Mahabharat and Ramayan, and sang Bengali religious song. From her, Subash imbibed a nurturing spirit, looking for situations in which to help people in distress, preferring gardening around the house to joining in sports with other boys. His father, who was reserved in manner in manner and busy with professional life, was a distant presence in a large family, causing Subhas to feel he had a nondescript childhood. Still, Janakinath read English literature avidly- John Milton, William Cowper, Mathhew Arnold and Shakespeare's Hamlet bieing among his favourites; several of his sons were to become English literature enthusiats like him.*

*In 1909 the 12 year-old Subhas followed his five brothers to the Ravenshaw Collegiate School in Cuttack. Here, Bengali and Sanskrit were also taught, as were ideas from Hindu scriptures such as the Vedas and the Upanishads not usually picked up at home. Although his western education continued apace, he began to wear Indian clothes and engaged with religious speculation. To his mother, he wrote long letters which displayed acquaintance with the ideas of the Bengali mystic Ramakrishna Paramahamsa and his disciple Swami Vivekananda, and the novel Ananda Math by Bankim Chandra Chatterjee, popular then among young Hindu men. Despite the preoccupation, Subhas was able to demonstrate an ability when needed to focus on his studies, to compete, and to succeed in exams. Im 1912, he secured the second position in the matriculation examination conducted under the auspices of the University of Calcutta.*

*Subhas followed his five brothers again in 1913 to Presindency College, Calcutta, the historic and traditional college for Bengal's upper-caste Hindu men. He chose to study philosophy, his readings including Krant, Hegel, Bergson and other Western philosophers. A year earlier, he had befriended Hemanta Kumar Sarkar, a confidant and partner in religious yearnings. At Presindency, their emtional ties grom stronger. In the fanciful language of religious imagery, they declared their pure love for each other. In the long vacations of 1914, they travelled to northern India for several months to search for a spiritual Guru to guide them. Subhas's family was not told clearly about the trip, leading them to think he had run away. During the trip, in which the guru proved elusive, Subhas came down with typhoid fever. His absense caused emotional distress to his parents, leading both parents to break down upon his return. Heated words were exchanged between Janakinath and Subhas. It took the return of Subhas's favourite brother, Sarat Chandra Bose, from law studies in England for the tempers to subside Subhas returned to presidency and busied himself with studies, debating and student journalism.*

*In February 1916, Bose was alleged to have masterminded or participated in an incident involving E.F. Oaten, Professor of History at Presidency. Before the incident, it was claimed by the students, Oaten had made rude remarks about Indian culture and collared and pushed some students; according to Oaten, the students were making an unacceptably loud noise just outside his class. A few days later, on 15 February, some students accosted Oaten on a stairway, surrounded him, beat him with sandals and took to flight. An inquiry committee was constituted. Although Oaten, who was unhurt, could not identify his assailants, a college servant testified too seeing Subhas Chandra Bose amog those fleeing, confirming for the authorities what they had determined to be the rumor among the students. Bose was expelled from the college and rusticated from University of Calcutta. The incident shocked Calcutta and caused anguish to Bose's family. He was ordered back to Cuttack. His family's connections were employed to pressure Ashutosh Mukherjee, thr Vice-Chancellor of Calcutta University. Despite this, Subhas Bose's expulsion remained in place until 20 July 1917, when the Syndicate of Calcutta University granted him permission to return, but to another college. He joined Scottish Church College, receiving his B.A. in 1918 in the First Class with honours in philosophy, placing second among all philosophy student in Calcutta University.*

*At his father's urging, Subhas agreed to travel to England to prepare and appear for the Indian Civil Services (ICS) examination. Arriving in London on 20 October 1919, Subhas readied his application for the ICS. For his references he put down Lord Sinha of Raipur, Under Secretary of State for India, and Bhupendranath Basu, a wealthy Calcutta lawyer who sat on the Council of India in London. Bose was eager also to gain admission to a college at the University of Cambridge. It was past the deadline for admission. He sought help from some Indian students and from the Non-Collegiate Students Board. The Board offered the university's education at an economical cost without formal admission to a college. Bose entered the register of the university on 19 November 1919 and simultaneously set about preparing for the Civil*

*Service exams. He chose the Mental and Moral Sciences Tripos at Cambridge, its completion requirement reduced to two years on account of his Indian B.A. There were six vacancies in the ICS. Subhas Bose took the open competitive exam for them in August 1920 and was placed fourth. This was a vital first step. Still remaining was a final examination in 1921 on more topics on India, including the Indian Penal Code, the Indian Evidence Act, Indian history and an Indian language. Successful candidates had also to clear a riding test. Having no fear of of these subjects and being a rider, Subhas felt the ICS was within easy reach. Yet between August 1920 and 1921 he began to have doubts about taking the final examination. Many letters were exchanged with his father and his brother Sarat Chandra Bose back in Calcutta. In one letter to Sarat, Subhas wrote,*

**"But for a man of my temperament who has been feeding on ideas that might be called eccentric - the line of least resistance is not the best line to follow... The uncertainties of life are not appaling to one who has not, at heart, worldly ambition. Moreover, it is not possible to serve one's country in the best and fullest manner if one is chained on to the civil service."**

*In April 1921, Subhas made his decision firm not to take the final examination for the ICS and wrote to Sarat informing him of the same, apologizing for the pain he would cause to his father, his mother and other members of his family. On 22 April 1921, he wrote to the Secretary of State for India, Edwin Montagu, starting,* **"I wish to have my name removed from the list of probationers in the Indian Civil Service."** *The following day he wrote again to Sarat:*

**"I received a letter from mother saying that in spite of what father and others think she prefers the ideals for which Mahatma Gandhi stands. I cannot tell you how happy I have been to receive such a letter. It will be worth a treasure for me as it has removed something like a burden from my mind."**

*For some time before Subhas had been in touch with C.R. Das, a lawyer who had risen to the helm of politics in Bengal; Das encouraged Subhas to return to Calcutta. With the ICS decision now firmly behind him, Subhas took his Cambridge B.A. Final examinations half-heartedly, passing, but being placed in the Third Class. He prepared to sail for India in June 1921, election for a fellow Indian student to pick up his diploma.*

## 1921-1932 : Indian National Congress

*Subhas Chandra Bose, aged 24, arrived ashore in India at Bombay on the morning of 16 July 1921 and immediately set about arranging an interview with Mahatma Gandhi. Gandhi, aged 51, was the the leader of the non-cooperation movement that had taken India by storm the previous year and in a quarter-century would envolve to secure its independence. Gandhi happened to be in Bombay and agreed to see Bose that afternoon. In Bose's account of the meeting, written many years later, he pilloried Gandhi with question after question. Bose thought Gandhi's answers were vague, his goals unclears, his plan for achieving them not thought through. Gandhi and Bose differed in this first meeting on the question of means -for Gandhi's non-violent means to any end were non-negotiable; in Bose's thought, all means were acceptable in the service of anti-colonial ends. They differed on the question of ends-Bose was attracted to totalitarian models of governance, which were anathematized by Gandhi. According to historian Gardon,* **"Gandhi, however, set Bose on to the leader of the Congress and Indian nationalism in Bengal, C.R. Das, and in him Bose found the leader whom he sought."** *Das was more flexible than Gandhi, more sympathetic to the extremism that had attracted idealistic young men such as Bose in Bengal. Das launched Bose into nationalist politics. Bose would work within the ambit of the Indian National Congress politics for nearly 20 years even as he tried to change its course.*

*In 1922, Bose founded the newspaper* **'Swaraj'** *and assumed charge of the publicity for the Bengal Provincial Congress Committee. His mentor was Chittaranjan Das, a voice for aggressive nationalism in Bengal. In 1923, Bose was elected the President of Indian Yoth Congress and also the Secretary of the Bengal State Congress. He became the editor of the newspaper* **'Forward'**, *which had been founded Chittaranjan Das. Subhas worked as the CEO of the Calcutta Municipal Corporation for Das when the* *latter was elected mayor of Calcutta in 1924. During the same year, when Subhas was leading a protest march in Calcutta, he, Maghfoor Ahmad Ajazi and other leaders were arrested and imprisoned. After a roundup of nationalists in 1925, Bose was sent to prison in Mandalay, British Burma, where he contracted tuberculosis.*

*In 1927, after being released from prison, Subhas became general secretary of the Congress party and worked with Jawaharlal Nehru for indepence. In late December 1928, Bose organised the Annual Meeting of the Indian National Congress in Calcutta. His most memorable role was as General officer commanding (GOC) Congress Volunteer Corps. A little later, Bose was again arrested and jailed for civil disobedience; this time he emerged to become Mayor of Calcutta in 1930.*

## 1933-1937 : Illness and Austria

*During the mid-1930s, Bose travelled in Europe, visiting Indian students and European politicians, including Benito Mussolini. He observed party organisation and saw communism and facism in action. In this period, he also researched and wrote the first part of his book* **The Indian Struggle***, which covered the country's independence movement in the years 1920-1934. Although it was published in London in 1935, the British government banned the book in the colony out of fears that it would encourage unrest. Bose was supported in Europe by the Indian*

*Central European Society organized by Otto Faltis from Vienna.*

## 1937-1940 : Indian National Congress

*In 1938, Bose stated his opinion that INC (Indian National Congress) "should be organized on the broadest anti-imperialist front with two-fold objective of winning political freedom and the establishment of a socialist regime. By 1938, Bose had become a leader of national stature and agreed to accept nomination as Congress President. He stood for unqualified Swaraj (self-governance), including the use of force against the British. This meant a confrontation with Mohandas Gandhi, who in fact opposed Bose's presidency, splitting the Indian National Congress party. Subhas attempted to maintain unity, but Gandhi advised Bose to form his own cabinet. The rift also divided Bose and Nehru; he appeared at the 1938 Congress meeting on a strecher. He was elected president again over Gandhi's preferred candidate Pattabhi Sitaramayya. U. Muthuramalingam Thevar strongly supported Bose in the intra-Congress dispute. Thevar mobilised all South India votes for Bose. However, due to the manoeuvrings of the Gandhi-led clique in the Congress Working Committee, Bose found himself forced to resign from the Congress presidency.*

*On 22 June 1939, Bose organised the All India Forward Bloc, a faction within the Indian National Congress, aimed at consolidating the political left, but it's main strength was in his home state, Bengal. U. Muthuramalingam Thevar, who was a staunch supporter of Bose from the beginning, joined the Forward Bloc. When Bose visited Madurai on 6 September, Thevar organized a massive rally as his reception.*

*When Bose was heading to Madurai, on a invitation of Thevar to a mass support for the Forward Bloc, he passed through Madras and spent three days at Gandhi Peak. His corresponding reveals that despite his clear dislike British subjugation, he was deeply impressed by methodical and systematic approach and their steadfastily disciplinarian outlook towrads life. In England, he exchanged ideas on the future of India with British Labour Party leaders and political thinkers like Lord Halifax, George Lansbury, Clement Attlee, Arthur Greenwood, Harold Laski, J.B.S. Haldane, Ivor Jennings, G.D.H. Cole, Gilbert Murray and Staffod Cripps.*

*He came to believe that an independent India need authoritarianism, on the lines of Turkey's Kemal Ataturk, for atleast two decades. For political reasons, Bose was refused permission by the British authorities to meet Ataturk at Ankara. During his sojourn in England Bose tried to schedule appointments with several politicians, but only the Labour Party and Liberal politicians agreed to meet with him. Conservation party officials refused to meet him or show him courtesy because he was a politician coming from a colony. In the 1930s leading figures in the Conservation Party had opposd even Dominion status for India. It was during the Labour Party government of 1945-1951, with Attlee as the Prime Minister, that India gained independence.*

*On the outbreak of war, Bose advocated a campaign of mass civil disobidience to protest against Viceroy Lord Linlithgrow's decision to declare war on India's behalf without consulting the Congress leadership. Having failed to persuade Gandhi of the necessity of this, Bose organized mass protest in Calcutta calling for the removal of the "Holwell Monuent", which then stood at the corner of Dalhousie Square in memoriam of those who died in the Black Hole of Calcutta. He was thrown in jail by the British, but was released following a seven-day hunger strike. Bose's house in Calcutta was kept under surveillance by CID.*

## 1941: Escape to Nazi Germany

*Bose's arrest and subsequent release set the scene for his escape to Nazi Germany, via Afghanistan and the Soviet Union. A few days before his escape, he sought solitude and, on this pretext, avoided meeting British guards and grew a beard. Late night 16 January 1941, the night of his escape, he dressed as a Pathan (brown long coat, a black fez-type coat and broad pyjamas) to avoid being identified. Bose escaped from under British surveillance from his Elgin Road house in Calcutta on the night of 17 January 1941, accompanied by his nephew Sisir Kumar Bose, later reaching Gomoh Railway Station (now Netaji Subhas Chandra Bose Gomoh Station) in the then state of*

*Bihar (now Jharkhand), India.*

*Bose journeyed to Peshawar with the help of the Abwehr, where he was met by Akbar Shah, Mohammed Shah and Bhagat Ram Talwar. Bose was taken to the home of Abad Khan, a trusted friend of Akbar Shah's. On 26 January 1941, Bose began his journey to reach Russia through British India's North West frontier with Afghanistan. For this reason, he enlisted the help of Mian Akbar Shah, then a Forward Bloc leader in the North-West Frontier Province. Shah had been out of India en route to the Soviet Union, and suggested a novel disguise for Bose to assume. Since Bose could not speak one word of Pashto, it would make him an easy target of Pashto speakers working for the British. For this reason, Shah suggested that Bose act deaf and dumb, and let his beard grow to mimic those of the tribesmen. Bose's guide Bhagat Ram Talwar, unknown to him, was a Soviet agent.*

*Supporters of the Aga Khan III helped him across the border into Afghanistan where he was met by an Abwehr unit posing as a party of road construction engineers from the Organization Todt who then aided his passage across Afghanistan via Kabul to the border with the Soviet Union. After assuming the guise of a Pashtun insurance agent ("Ziaudddin") to reach Afghanistan, Bose changed his guise and travelled to Moscow on the Italian passport of an Italian nobleman "Count Orlando Mazzotta". From Moscow, he reached Rome, and from there he travelled to Nazi Germany. Once in Russia the NKVD transported Bose to Moscow where he hoped that Russia's historical enmity to British rule in India would result in support for his plans for a popular rising in India. However, Bose found the Soviets' response disappointing and was rapidly passed over to the German Ambassador in Moscow, Count von der Schulenburg. He had Bose flown on to Berlin in a special courier aircraft at the beginning of April where he was to receive a more favourable hearing from Joachim von Ribbentrop and the Foreign Ministry officials at the Wilhelmstrasse.*

## 1941–1943: Collaboration with Nazi Germany

*In Germany, Bose was attached to the Special Bureau for India under Adam von Trott zu Solz which was responsible for broadcasting on the German-sponsored Azad Hind Radio. He founded the Free India Center in Berlin, and created the Indian Legion (consisting of some 4500 soldiers) out of Indian prisoners of war who had previously fought for the British in North Africa prior to their capture by Axis forces. The Indian Legion was attached to the Wehrmacht, and later transferred to the Waffen SS. Its members swore the following allegiance to Hitler and Bose: "I swear by God this holy oath that I will obey the leader of the German race and state, Adolf Hitler, as the commander of the German armed forces in the fight for India, whose leader is Subhas Chandra Bose". This oath clearly abrogated control of the Indian legion to the German armed forces whilst stating Bose's overall leadership of India. He was also, however, prepared to envisage an invasion of*

*India via the USSR by Nazi troops, spearheaded by the Azad Hind Legion; many have questioned his judgment here, as it seems unlikely that the Germans could have been easily persuaded to leave after such an invasion, which might also have resulted in an Axis victory in the War.*

*Soon, according to historian Romain Hayes, "the (German) Foreign Office procured a luxurious residence for (Bose) along with a butler, cook, gardener, and an SS-chauffeured car. Emilie Schenkl moved in openly with him. The Germans, aware of the nature of the relationship, refrained from any involvement." However, most of the staff in the Special Bureau for India, which had been set up to aid Bose, did not get along with Emilie. In particular Adam von Trott, Alexander Werth and Freda Kretschemer, according to historian Leonard A. Gordon, "appear to have disliked her intensely. They believed that she and Bose were not married and that she was using her liaison with Bose to live an especially comfortable life during the hard times of war" and that differences were compounded by issues of class. In November 1942, Schenkl gave birth to their daughter.*

*The Germans were unwilling to form an alliance with Bose because they considered him unpopular in comparison with Mahatma Gandhi and Jawaharlal Nehru. By the spring of 1942, the German army was mired in the USSR. Bose, due to disappointment over the lack of response from Nazi Germany, was now keen to move to Southeast Asia, where Japan had just won quick victories. However, he still expected official recognition from Nazi Germany. Adolf Hitler during his only meeting with Bose in late May 1942 refused to entertain Bose's requests and facilitated him with a submarine voyage to East Asia.*

*In February 1943, Bose left Schenkl and their baby daughter and boarded a German submarine to travel, via transfer to a Japanese submarine, to Japanese-occupied southeast Asia. In all, 3,000 Indian prisoners of war signed up for the Free India Legion. But instead of being delighted, Bose was worried. A left-wing admirer of Russia, he was devastated when Hitler's tanks rolled across the Soviet border. Matters were worsened by the fact that the now-retreating German army would be in no position to offer him help in driving the British from India. When he met Hitler in May 1942, his suspicions were confirmed, and he came to believe that the Nazi leader was more interested in using his men to win propaganda victories than military ones. So, in February 1943, Bose boarded a German U-boat and left for Japan. This left the men he had recruited leaderless and demoralised in Germany.*

## 1943–1945: Japanese-occupied Asia

*In 1943, after being disillusioned that Germany could be of any help in gaining India's independence, Bose left for Japan. He travelled with the German submarine U-180 around the Cape of Good Hope to the southeast of Madagascar, where he was transferred to the I-29 for the rest of the journey to Imperial Japan. This was the only civilian transfer between two submarines of two different navies in World War II.*

*The Indian National Army (INA) was the brainchild of Japanese Major (and post-war Lieutenant-General) Iwaichi Fujiwara, head of the Japanese intelligence unit Fujiwara Kikan. Fujiwara's mission was "to raise an army which would fight alongside the Japanese army." He first met Pritam Singh Dhillon, the president of the Bangkok chapter of the Indian Independence League, and through Pritam Singh's network recruited a captured British Indian army captain, Mohan Singh, on the western Malayan peninsula in December 1941. The First Indian National Army was formed as a result of discussion between Fujiwara and Mohan Singh in the second half of December 1941, and the name chosen jointly by them in the first week of January 1942.*

*This was along the concept of, and with support of, what was then known as the Indian Independence League headed from Tokyo by expatriate nationalist leader Rash Behari Bose. The first INA was however disbanded in December 1942 after disagreements between the Hikari Kikan and Mohan Singh, who came to believe that the Japanese High Command was using the INA as a mere pawn and propaganda tool. Singh was taken into custody and the troops returned to the prisoner-of-war camp. However, the idea of an independence army was revived with the arrival of Subhas Chandra Bose in the Far East in 1943. In July, at a meeting in Singapore, Rash Behari Bose handed over control of the organisation to Subhas Chandra Bose. Bose was able to reorganise the fledgling army and organise massive support among the expatriate Indian population in south-east Asia, who lent their support by both enlisting in the Indian National Army, as well as financially in response to Bose's calls for sacrifice for the independence cause. INA had a separate women's unit, the Rani of Jhansi Regiment (named after Rani Lakshmi Bai) headed by Capt. Lakshmi Swaminathan, which is seen as a first of its kind in Asia.Even when faced with military reverses, Bose was able to maintain support for the Azad Hind movement. Spoken as a part of a motivational speech for the Indian National Army at a rally of Indians in Burma on 4 July 1944, Bose's most famous quote was "Give me blood, and I shall give you freedom!" In this, he urged the people of India to join him in his fight against the British Raj. Spoken in Hindi, Bose's words are highly evocative. The troops of the INA were under the aegis of a provisional government, the Azad Hind Government, which came to produce its own currency, postage stamps, court and civil code, and was recognised by nine Axis states—Germany, Japan, Italian Social Republic, the Independent State of Croatia, the Wang Jingwei regime in Nanjing, China, a provisional government of Burma, Manchukuo and Japanese-controlled Philippines. Of those countries, five were authorities established under Axis occupation. This government participated in the so-called Greater East Asia Conference as an observer in November 1943.*

*The INA's first commitment was in the Japanese thrust towards Eastern Indian frontiers of Manipur. INA's special forces, the Bahadur Group, were involved in operations behind enemy lines both during the diversionary attacks in Arakan, as well as the Japanese thrust towards Imphal and Kohima.*

*The Japanese also took possession of Andaman and Nicobar Islands in 1942 and a year later, the Provisional Government and the INA were established in the Andaman and Nicobar Islands with Lt Col. Arcot Doraiswamy Loganadan appointed its Governor General. The islands were renamed Shaheed (Martyr) and Swaraj (Independence). However, the Japanese Navy remained in essential control of the island's administration. During Bose's only visit to the islands in early 1944, apparently in the interest of shielding Bose from attaining a full knowledge of ultimate Japanese intentions, his Japanese hosts carefully isolated him from the local population. At that time the island's Japanese administration had been torturing the leader of the island's Indian Independence League, Diwan Singh, who later died of his injuries in the Cellular Jail. During Bose's visit to the islands several locals attempted to alert Bose to Singh's plight, but apparently without success. During this time Loganathan became aware of his lack of any genuine administrative control and resigned in protest as Governor General, later returning to the Government's headquarters in Rangoon.*

*On the Indian mainland, an Indian Tricolour flag, modelled after that of the Indian National Congress, was raised for the first time in the town of Moirang, in Manipur, in north-eastern India. The adjacent towns of Kohima and Imphal were then encircled and placed under siege by divisions of the Japanese Army, working in conjunction with the Burmese National Army, and with Brigades of the INA, known as the Gandhi and Nehru Brigades. This attempt at conquering the Indian mainland had the Axis codename of Operation U-Go.*

*During this operation, on 6 July 1944, in a speech broadcast by the Azad Hind Radio from Singapore, Bose addressed Mahatma Gandhi as the "Father of the Nation" and asked for his blessings and good wishes for the war he was fighting. This was the first time that Gandhi was referred to by this appellation. The protracted Japanese attempts to take these two towns depleted Japanese resources, with Operation U-Go ultimately proving unsuccessful. Through several months of Japanese onslaught on these two towns, Commonwealth forces remained entrenched in the towns. Commonwealth forces then counter-attacked, inflicting serious losses on the Axis led forces, who were then forced into a retreat back into Burmese territory. After the Japanese defeat at the battles of Kohima and Imphal, Bose's Provisional Government's aim of establishing a base in mainland India was lost forever.*

*Still the INA fought in key battles against the British Indian Army in Burmese territory, notable in Meiktilla, Mandalay, Pegu, Nyangyu and Mount Popa. However, with the fall of Rangoon, Bose's government ceased to be an effective political entity. A large proportion of the INA troops surrendered under Lt Col Loganathan. The remaining troops retreated with Bose towards Malaya or made for Thailand. Japan's surrender at the end of the war also led to the surrender of the remaining elements of the Indian National Army. The INA prisoners were then repatriated to India and some tried for treason.*

## 18 August 1945: Death

*Subhas Chandra Bose died on 18 August 1945 from third-degree burns after his airplane crashed in Japanese-ruled Formosa (now Taiwan). However, many among his supporters, especially in Bengal, refused at the time, and have refused since, to believe either the fact or the circumstances of his death. Conspiracy theories appeared within hours of his death and have thereafter had a long shelf life, keeping alive various martial myths about Bose.*

*In Taihoku, at around 2:30 PM as the bomber with Bose on board was leaving the standard path taken by aircraft during take-off, the passengers inside heard a loud sound, similar to an engine backfiring. The mechanics on the tarmac saw something fall out of the plane. It was the portside engine, or a part of it, and the propeller. The plane swung wildly to the right and plummeted, crashing, breaking into two, and exploding into flames. Inside, the chief pilot, copilot and Lieutenant-General Tsunamasa Shidei, the Vice Chief of Staff of the Japanese Kwantung*

*Army, who was to have made the negotiations for Bose with the Soviet army in Manchuria, were instantly killed. Bose's assistant Habibur Rahman was stunned, passing out briefly, and Bose, although conscious and not fatally hurt, was soaked in gasoline. When Rahman came to, he and Bose attempted to leave by the rear door, but found it blocked by the luggage. They then decided to run through the flames and exit from the front. The ground staff, now approaching the plane, saw two people staggering towards them, one of whom had become a human torch. The human torch turned out to be Bose, whose gasoline-soaked clothes had instantly ignited. Rahman and a few others managed to smother the flames, but also noticed that Bose's face and head appeared badly burned. According to Joyce Chapman Lebra, "A truck which served as ambulance rushed Bose and the other passengers to the Nanmon Military Hospital south of Taihoku." The airport personnel called Dr. Taneyoshi Yoshimi, the surgeon-in-charge at the hospital at around 3 PM. Bose was conscious and mostly coherent when they reached the hospital, and for some time thereafter. Bose was naked, except for a blanket wrapped around him, and Dr. Yoshimi immediately saw evidence of third-degree burns on many parts of the body, especially on his chest, doubting very much that he would live.[130] Dr. Yoshimi promptly began to treat Bose and was assisted by Dr. Tsuruta. According to historian Leonard A. Gordon, who interviewed all the hospital personnel later*

*Soon, in spite of the treatment, Bose went into a coma. A few hours later, between 9 and 10 PM (local time) on Saturday, 18 August 1945, Bose died aged 48.*

*Bose's body was cremated in the main Taihoku crematorium two days later, 20 August 1945. On 23 August 1945, the Japanese news agency Do Trzei announced the death of Bose and Shidea. On 7 September a Japanese officer, Lieutenant Tatsuo Hayashida, carried Bose's ashes to Tokyo, and the following morning they were handed to the president of the Tokyo Indian Independence League, Rama Murti. On 14 September a memorial service was held for Bose in Tokyo and a few days later the ashes were turned over to the priest of the Renkōji Temple of Nichiren Buddhism in Tokyo. There they have remained ever since.*

*Among the INA personnel, there was widespread disbelief, shock, and trauma. Most affected were the young Tamil Indians from Malaya and Singapore, both men and women, who comprised the bulk of the civilians who had enlisted in the INA. The professional soldiers in the INA, most of whom were Punjabis, faced an uncertain future, with many fatalistically expecting reprisals from the British. In India the Indian National Congress's official line was succinctly expressed in a letter Mohandas Karamchand (Mahatma) Gandhi wrote to Rajkumari Amrit Kaur. Said Gandhi, "Subhas Bose has died well. He was undoubtedly a patriot, though misguided." Many congressmen had not forgiven Bose for quarrelling with Gandhi and for collaborating with what they considered was Japanese fascism. The*

*Indian soldiers in the British Indian army, some two and a half million of whom had fought during the Second World War, were conflicted about the INA. Some saw the INA as traitors and wanted them punished; others felt more sympathetic. The British Raj, though never seriously threatened by the INA, tried 300 INA officers for treason in the INA trials, but eventually backtracked.*

## Ideology

*Subhas Chandra Bose believed that the Bhagavad Gita was a great source of inspiration for the struggle against the British. Swami Vivekananda's teachings on universalism, his nationalist thoughts and his emphasis on social service and reform had all inspired Subhas Chandra Bose from his very young days. The fresh interpretation of India's ancient scriptures had appealed immensely to him. Some scholars think that Hindu spirituality formed an essential part of his political and social thought. As historian Leonard Gordon explains "Inner religious explorations continued to be a part of his adult life. This set him apart from the slowly growing number of atheistic socialists and communists who dotted the Indian landscape."*

# BHAGAT SINGH

**Summary:**

*Bhagat Singh was an Indian anti-colonial revolutionary, who participated in the mistaken murder of a junior British police officer in December 1928 in what was to be retaliation for the death of an Indian nationalist. He later took part in a largely symbolic bombing of the Central Legislative Assembly in Delhi and a hunger strike in jail, which-on the back of sympathetic coverage in Indian-owned newspapers-turned him into a household name in the Punjab region, and after his execution at age 23 into a martyr and folk hero in Northern India. Borrowing ideas from Bolshevism and anarchism, the charismatic Singh electrified a growing militancy in India in the 1930s, and prompted urgent introspection within the Indian National Congress's nonviolent but eventually successful campaign for India's independence.*

**BHAGAT SINGH**

## Early Life

*Bhagat Singh was born into a Punjabi Jat Sikh family on 27 September 1907 in the village of Banga in the Lyallpur district of the Punjab in what was then British India and is today Pakistan; he was the second of seven children—four sons, and three daughters—born to Vidyavati and her husband Kishan Singh Sandhu. Bhagat Singh's father and his uncle Ajit Singh were active in progressive politics, taking part in the agitation around the Canal Colonization Bill in 1907, and later the Ghadar Movement of 1914–1915.*

*After being sent to the village school in Banga for a few years, Bhagat Singh was enrolled in the Dayanand Anglo-Vedic School in Lahore. In 1923, he joined the National College in Lahore, founded two years earlier by Lala Lajpat Rai in response to Mahatma Gandhi's non-cooperation movement, which urged Indian students to shun schools and colleges subsidized by the British Indian government.*

*Police became concerned with Singh's influence on youths and arrested him in May 1927 on the pretext that he had been involved in a bombing that had taken place in Lahore in October 1926. He was released on a surety of Rs. 60,000 five weeks after his arrest. He wrote for, and edited, Urdu and Punjabi newspapers, published in Amritsar and also contributed to low-priced pamphlets published by the Naujawan Bharat Sabha that excoriated the British. He also wrote for*

*Kirti, the journal of the Kirti Kisan Party ("Workers and Peasants Party") and briefly for the Veer Arjun newspaper, published in Delhi. He often used pseudonyms, including names such as Balwant, Ranjit and Vidhrohi.*

## Revolutionary Activities

### *Killing of John Saunders:*

*In 1928, the British government set up the Simon Commission to report on the political situation in India. Some Indian political parties boycotted the Commission because there were no Indians in its membership, and there were protests across the country. When the Commission visited Lahore on 30 October 1928, Lala Lajpat Rai led a march in protest against it. Police attempts to disperse the large crowd resulted in violence. The superintendent of police, James A. Scott, ordered the police to lathi charge (use batons against) the protesters and personally assaulted Rai, who was injured. Rai died of a heart attack on 17 November 1928. Doctors thought that his death might have been hastened by the injuries he had received. When the matter was raised in the Parliament of the United Kingdom, the British Government denied any role in Rai's death.*

*Singh was a prominent member of the Hindustan Republican Association (HRA) and was probably responsible, in large part, for its change of name to*

*Hindustan Socialist Republican Association (HSRA) in 1928. The HSRA vowed to avenge Rai's death. Singh conspired with revolutionaries like Shivaram Rajguru, Sukhdev Thapar, and Chandrashekhar Azad to kill Scott. However, in a case of mistaken identity, the plotters shot John P. Saunders, an Assistant Superintendent of Police, as he was leaving the District Police Headquarters in Lahore on 17 December 1928.*

*Contemporary reaction to the killing differs substantially from the adulation that later surfaced. The Naujawan Bharat Sabha, which had organised the Lahore protest march along with the HSRA, found that attendance at its subsequent public meetings dropped sharply. Politicians, activists, and newspapers, including The People, which Rai had founded in 1925, stressed that non-co-operation was preferable to violence. The murder was condemned as a retrograde action by Mahatma Gandhi, the Congress leader, but Jawaharlal Nehru later wrote that:*

**"Bhagat Singh did not become popular because of his act of terrorism but because he seemed to vincidate, for the moment, the honour of Lala Lajpat Rai, and through himof the nation."**

## Escape from Lahore

*Bhagat Singh and Rajguru, both carrying loaded revolvers, left the house early the next day. Dressed in western attire (Bhagat Singh cut his hair, shaved his beard and wore a hat over cropped hair), and carrying Devi's sleeping child, Singh and Devi passed as a young couple, while Rajguru carried their luggage as their servant. At the station, Singh managed to conceal his identity while buying tickets, and the three boarded the train heading to Cawnpore (now Kanpur). There they boarded a train for Lucknow since the CID at Howrah railway station usually scrutinised passengers on the direct train from Lahore. At Lucknow, Rajguru left separately for Benares while Singh, Devi and the infant went to Howrah, with all except Singh returning to Lahore a few days later.*

## Delhi Assembly bombing and arrest

*For some time, Bhagat Singh had been exploiting the power of drama as a means to inspire the revolt against the British, purchasing a magic lantern to show slides that enlivened his talks about revolutionaries such as Ram Prasad Bismil who had died as a result of the Kakori conspiracy. In 1929, he proposed a dramatic act to the HSRA intended to gain massive publicity for their aims. Influenced by Auguste Vaillant, a French anarchist who had bombed the Chamber of Deputies in Paris, Singh's plan was to explode a bomb inside the Central Legislative*

*Assembly. The nominal intention was to protest against the Public Safety Bill, and the Trade Dispute Act, which had been rejected by the Assembly but were being enacted by the Viceroy using his special powers; the actual intention was for the perpetrators to allow themselves to be arrested so that they could use court appearances as a stage to publicise their cause.*

*The HSRA leadership was initially opposed to Bhagat's participation in the bombing because they were certain that his prior involvement in the Saunders shooting meant that his arrest would ultimately result in his execution. However, they eventually decided that he was their most suitable candidate. On 8 April 1929, Singh, accompanied by Batukeshwar Dutt, threw two bombs into the Assembly chamber from its public gallery while it was in session. The bombs had been designed not to kill, but some members, including George Ernest Schuster, the finance member of the Viceroy's Executive Council, were injured. The smoke from the bombs filled the Assembly so that Singh and Dutt could probably have escaped in the confusion had they wished. Instead, they stayed shouting the slogan "Inquilab Zindabad!" ("Long Live the Revolution") and threw leaflets. The two men were arrested and subsequently moved through a series of jails in Delhi.*

## Assembly case trial

*"Public criticism of this terrorist action was unequivocal." Gandhi, once again, issued strong words of disapproval of their deed. Nonetheless, the jailed Bhagat was reported to be elated, and referred to the subsequent legal proceedings as a "drama". Bhagat Singh and Dutt eventually responded to the criticism by writing the Assembly Bomb Statement:*

*"Wehold human life sacred beyond words. We are neither perpetrators of dastardly outrages ... nor are we 'lunatics' as the Tribune of Lahore and some others would have it believed ... Force when aggressively applied is 'violence' and is, therefore, morally unjustifiable, but when it is used in the furtherance of a legitimate cause, it has its moral justification."*

*The trial began in the first week of June, following a preliminary hearing in May. On 12 June, both men were sentenced to life imprisonment for: "causing explosions of a nature likely to endanger life, unlawfully and maliciously." Dutt had been defended by Asaf Ali, while Singh defended himself. Doubts have been raised about the accuracy of testimony offered at the trial. One key discrepancy concerns the automatic pistol that Singh had been carrying when he was arrested. Some witnesses said that he had fired two or three shots while the police sergeant who arrested him testified that the gun was pointed downward when he took it from him and that Singh "was playing with it." According to an article in the India Law Journal, the prosecution witnesses were coached, their accounts were incorrect, and Singh had turned over the pistol himself. Singh was given a life sentence.*

## Arrest of associates

*In 1929, the HSRA had set up bomb factories in Lahore and Saharanpur. On 15 April 1929, the Lahore bomb factory was discovered by the police, leading to the arrest of other members of HSRA, including Sukhdev, Kishori Lal, and Jai Gopal. Not long after this, the Saharanpur factory was also raided and some of the conspirators became informants. With the new information available, the police were able to connect the three strands of the Saunders murder, Assembly bombing, and bomb manufacture. Bhagat Singh, Sukhdev, Rajguru, and 21 others were charged with the Saunders murder.*

## Hunger strike and Lahore conspiracy case

*Bhagat Singh was re-arrested for murdering Saunders and Chanan Singh based on substantial evidence against him, including statements by his associates, Hans Raj Vohra and Jai Gopal. His life sentence in the Assembly Bomb case was deferred until the Saunders case was decided. He was sent to Central Jail*

*Mianwali from the Delhi jail. There he witnessed discrimination between European and Indian prisoners. He considered himself, along with others, to be a political prisoner. He noted that he had received an enhanced diet at Delhi which was not being provided at Mianwali. He led other Indian, self-identified political prisoners he felt were being treated as common criminals in a hunger strike. They demanded equality in food standards, clothing, toiletries, and other hygienic necessities, as well as access to books and a daily newspaper. They argued that they should not be forced to do manual labour or any undignified work in the jail.*

*The hunger strike inspired a rise in public support for Singh and his colleagues from around June 1929. The Tribune newspaper was particularly prominent in this movement and reported on mass meetings in places such as Lahore and Amritsar. The government had to apply Section 144 of the criminal code in an attempt to limit gatherings.*

*Jawaharlal Nehru met Bhagat Singh and the other strikers in Central Jail Mianwali. After the meeting he stated:*

**"I was very much pained to see the distress of the heroes. They have staked their lives in this struggle. They want that political prisoners should be treated as political prisoners. I am quite hopeful that their sacrifice would be crowned with success."**

*Muhammad Ali Jinnah spoke in support of the strikers in the Assembly, saying:*

**"The man who goes on hunger strike has a soul. He is moved by that soul, and he believes in the justice of his cause ... however much you deplore them and, however, much you say they are misguided, it is the system, this damnable system of governance, which is resented by the people."**

*The government tried to break the strike by placing different food items in the prison cells to test the prisoners' resolve. Water pitchers were filled with milk so that either the prisoners remained thirsty or broke their strike; nobody faltered and the impasse continued. The authorities then attempted force-feeding the prisoners but this was resisted. With the matter still unresolved, the Indian Viceroy, Lord Irwin, cut short his vacation in Simla to discuss the situation with jail authorities. Since the activities of the hunger strikers had gained popularity and attention amongst the people nationwide, the government decided to advance the start of the Saunders murder trial, which was henceforth called the Lahore Conspiracy Case. Singh was transported to Borstal Jail, Lahore, and the trial began there on 10 July 1929. In addition to charging them with the murder of Saunders, Singh and the 27 other prisoners were charged with plotting a conspiracy to murder Scott, and waging a war against the King. Singh, still on hunger strike, had to be carried to the court handcuffed on a stretcher; he had lost 14 pounds (6.4 kg) from his original weight of 133 pounds (60 kg) since beginning the strike.*

*The government was beginning to make concessions but refused to move on the core issue of recognising the classification of "political prisoner". In the eyes of officials, if someone broke the law then that was a personal act, not a political one, and they were common criminals. By now, the condition of another hunger striker, Jatindra Nath Das, lodged in the same jail, had deteriorated considerably. The Jail committee recommended his unconditional release, but the government rejected the suggestion and offered to release him on bail. On 13 September 1929, Das died after a 63-day hunger strike. Almost all the nationalist leaders in the country paid tribute to Das' death. Mohammad Alam and Gopi Chand Bhargava resigned from the Punjab Legislative Council in protest, and Nehru moved a successful adjournment motion in the Central Assembly as a censure against the "inhumane treatment" of the Lahore prisoners. Singh finally heeded a resolution of the Congress party, and a request by his father, ending his hunger strike on 5 October 1929 after 116 days.[44] During this period, Singh's popularity among common Indians extended beyond Punjab.*

*Singh's attention now turned to his trial, where he was to face a Crown prosecution team comprising C. H. Carden-Noad, Kalandar Ali Khan, Jai Gopal Lal, and the prosecuting inspector, Bakshi Dina Nath. The defence was composed of eight lawyers. Prem Dutt Verma, the youngest amongst the 27 accused, threw his slipper at Gopal when he turned and became a prosecution witness in court. As a result, the magistrate ordered that all the accused should be handcuffed. Singh and others refused to be handcuffed and were subjected to brutal beating. The revolutionaries refused to attend the court and Singh wrote a letter to the magistrate citing various reasons for their refusal. The magistrate ordered the trial to proceed without the accused or members of the HSRA. This was a setback for Singh as he could no longer use the trial as a forum to publicise his views.*

## Special Tribunal

*To speed up the slow trial, the Viceroy, Lord Irwin, declared an emergency on 1 May 1930 and introduced an ordinance to set up a special tribunal composed of three high court judges for the case. This decision cut short the normal process of justice as the only appeal after the tribunal was to the Privy Council located in England. On 2 July 1930, a habeas corpus petition was filed in the High Court challenging the ordinance on the grounds that it was ultra vires and, therefore, illegal; the Viceroy had no powers to shorten the customary process of determining justice. The petition argued that the Defence of India Act 1915 allowed the Viceroy to introduce an ordinance, and set up such a tribunal, only under conditions of a breakdown of law-and-order, which, it was claimed in this case, had not occurred. However, the petition was dismissed as being premature. Carden-Noad presented the government's charges of conducting robberies, and the illegal acquisition of arms and ammunition among others. The evidence of G. T. H. Hamilton Harding, the Lahore superintendent of police, shocked the court. He stated that he had filed the first information report against the accused under specific orders from the chief secretary to the governor of Punjab and that he was unaware of the details of the case. The prosecution depended mainly on the evidence of P. N. Ghosh, Hans Raj Vohra, and Jai Gopal who had been Singh's associates in the HSRA. On 10 July 1930, the tribunal decided to press charges against only 15 of the 18 accused and allowed their petitions to be taken up for hearing the next day. The trial ended on 30 September 1930. The three accused, whose charges were withdrawn, included Dutt who had already been given a life sentence in the Assembly bomb case. The ordinance (and the tribunal) would lapse on 31 October 1930 as it had not been passed by the Central Assembly or the British Parliament. On 7 October 1930, the tribunal delivered its 300-page judgement based on all the evidence and concluded that the participation of Singh, Sukhdev , and Shivaram Rajguru in Saunder's murder was proven. They were sentenced to death by hanging. Of the other accused, three were acquitted (Ajoy Ghosh, Jatindra Nath Sanyal and Des Raj) Kundan Lal received seven years' rigorous imprisonment, Prem Dutt received five years of the same, and the remaining seven Kishori Lal, Mahavir Singh, Bijoy Kumar Sinha, Shiv Verma, Gaya Prasad, Jaidev Kapoor and Kamal Nath Tewari were all sentenced to transportation for life.*

## Appeal to the Privy Council

*In Punjab province, a defence committee drew up a plan to appeal to the Privy Council. Singh was initially against the appeal but later agreed to it in the hope that the appeal would popularise the HSRA in Britain. The appellants claimed that the ordinance which created the tribunal was invalid while the government countered that the Viceroy was completely empowered to create such a tribunal. The appeal was dismissed by Judge Viscount Dunedin.*

## Reactions to the judgement

*After the rejection of the appeal to the Privy Council, Congress party president Madan Mohan Malaviya filed a mercy appeal before Irwin on 14 February 1931. Some prisoners sent Mahatma Gandhi an appeal to intervene. In his notes dated 19 March 1931, the Viceroy recorded:*

**"While returning Gandhiji asked me if he could talk about the case of Bhagat Singh because newspapers had come out with the news of his slated hanging on March 24th. It would be a very unfortunate day because on that day the new president of the Congress had to reach Karachi and there would be a lot of hot discussion. I explained to him that I had given a very careful thought to it but I did**

*not find any basis to convince myself to commute the sentence. It appeared he found my reasoning weighty."*

*The Communist Party of Great Britain expressed its reaction to the case:*

*"The history of this case, of which we do not come across any example in relation to the political cases, reflects the symptoms of callousness and cruelty which is the outcome of bloated desire of the imperialist government of Britain so that fear can be instilled in the hearts of the repressed people."*

*A plan to rescue Singh and fellow HSRA inmates from the jail failed. HSRA member Durga Devi's husband, Bhagwati Charan Vohra, attempted to manufacture bombs for the purpose, but died when they exploded accidentally.*

*Execution*

*Bhagat Singh, Rajguru and Sukhdev were sentenced to death in the Lahore conspiracy case and ordered to be hanged on 24 March 1931. The schedule was moved forward by 11 hours and the three were hanged on 23 March 1931 at 7:30 PM in the Lahore jail. It is reported that no magistrate at the time was willing to supervise Singh's hanging as was required by law. The execution was supervised instead by an honorary judge named Nawab Muhammad Ahmed Khan Kasuri, who also signed the three death warrants, as their original warrants had expired. The jail authorities then broke a hole in the rear wall of the jail, removed the bodies, and secretly cremated the three men under cover of darkness outside Ganda Singh Wala village, and then threw the ashes into the Sutlej river, about 10 kilometres (6.2 mi) from Ferozepore.*

## Criticism of the tribunal trial

*Bhagat Singh's trial has been described by the Supreme Court as "contrary to the fundamental doctrine of criminal jurisprudence" because there was no opportunity for the accused to defend themselves. The Special Tribunal was a departure from the normal procedure adopted for a trial and its decision could only be appealed to the Privy Council located in Britain. The accused were absent from the court and the judgement was passed ex-parte. The ordinance, which was introduced by the Viceroy to form the Special Tribunal, was never approved by the Central Assembly or the British Parliament, and it eventually lapsed without any legal or constitutional sanctity.*

## Reactions to the executions

*In the issue of Young India of 29 March 1931, Gandhi wrote:*

**"Bhagat Singh and his two associates have been hanged. The Congress made many attempts to save their lives and the Government entertained many hopes of it, but all has been in a vain."**

Bhagat Singh did not wish to live. He refused to apologise, or even file an appeal. Bhagat Singh was not a devotee of non-violence, but he did not subscribe to the religion of violence. He took to violence due to helplessness and to defend his homeland. In his last letter, Bhagat Singh wrote, " I have been arrested while waging a war. For me there can be no gallows. Put me into the mouth of a cannon and blow me off." These heroes had conquered the fear of death. Let us bow to them a thousand times for their heroism.

But we should not imitate their act. In our land of millions of destitute and crippled people, if we take to the practice of seeking justice through murder, there will be a terrifying situation. Our poor people will become victims of our atrocities. By making a dharma of violence, we shall be reaping the fruit of our own actions.

Hence, though we praise the courage of these brave men, we should never countenance their activities. Our dharma is to swallow our anger, abide by the discipline of non-violence and carry out our duty.

## Gandhi's role

On 23 March, Mahatama Gandhi had written a letter to viceroy appealing for commutation for the death sentences against Bhagat Singh, Sukhdev and Rajguru. While there have been unfounded claims that Gandhi had an opportunity to stop Singh's execution, it is held that Gandhi did not have enough influence with the British to stop the execution, much less arrange it, but that he did his best to save Singh's life. Gandhi supporters assert that Singh's role in the independence movement was no threat to Gandhi's role as its leader, so he would have no reason to want him dead. Gandhi always maintained that he was a great admirer of Singh's patriotism. He also stated that he was opposed to Singh's execution (and for that matter, capital punishment in general) and proclaimed that he had no power to stop it. Of Singh's execution Gandhi said: "The government certainly had the right to hang these men. However, there are some rights which do credit to those who possess them only if they are enjoyed in name only." Gandhi also once remarked about capital punishment: "I cannot in all conscience agree to anyone being sent to the gallows. God alone can take life, because he alone gives it." Gandhi had managed to have 90,000 political prisoners, who were not members of his Satyagraha movement, released under the Gandhi–Irwin Pact. According to a report in the Indian magazine Frontline, he did plead several times for the commutation of the death sentences of Singh, Rajguru and Sukhdev, including a personal visit on 19 March 1931. In a letter to the Viceroy on the day of their execution, he pleaded fervently for *commutation, not knowing that the letter would arrive too late.*

# CHAPTER THREE

# CHANDRA SHEKHAR AZAD

**Summary:**

*Chandra Shekhar Azad, was an Indian revolutionary who reorganised the Hindustan Republican Association (HRA) under its new name of Hindustan Socialist Republican Association (HSRA) after the death of its founder, Ram Prasad Bismil, and three other prominent party leaders, Roshan Singh, Rajendra Nath Lahiri and Ashfaqulla Khan. He hailed from Bardarka village in Unnao district of United Provinces and his parents were Sitaram Tiwari and Jagrani Devi. He often used the pseudonym "Balraj" while signing pamphlets issued as the commander-in-chief of the HSRA.*

**CHANDRA SHEKHAR AZAD**

## Life Before Revolution

*Chandra Shekhar Azad was born on 23 July 1906 in Bhabhra village as Chandra Shekhar Tiwari, in a Brahmin family, in the princely-state of Alirajpur. His forefathers were from Badarka village of Unnao district of Uttar Pradesh. His mother, Jagrani Devi, was the third wife of Sitaram Tiwari, whose previous wives had died young. After the birth of their first son, Sukhdev, in Badarka, the family moved to Alirajpur State.*

*His mother wanted her son to be a great Sanskrit scholar and persuaded his father to send him to Kashi Vidyapeeth at Banaras to study. In 1921, when the Non-Cooperation Movement was at its height, Chandra Shekhar, then a 15-year-old student, joined. As a result, he was arrested on 20 December. On being presented before the Parsi district magistrate Justice M. P. Khareghat a week later, he gave his name as "Azad" (The Free), his father's name as "Swatantrata" (Independence) and his residence as "Jail". The angered magistrate punished him with 15 lashes.*

## Revolutionary life

*After the suspension of the non-cooperation movement in 1922 by Mahatma Gandhi, Azad became disappointed. He met a young revolutionary, Manmath Nath Gupta, who introduced him to Ram*

*Prasad Bismil who had formed the Hindustan Republican Association (HRA), a revolutionary organization. He then became an active member of the HRA and started to collect funds for HRA. Most of the fund collection was through robberies of government property. He was involved in the Kakori Train Robbery of 1925, the shooting of John P. Saunders at Lahore in 1928 to avenge the killing of Lala Lajpat Rai, and at last, in the attempt to blow up the Viceroy of India's train in 1929.*

*Azad got to read Karl Marx's Manifesto of the Communist Party from his comrade Shiv Verma. When Azad was the commander-in-chief of the revolutionary party, he often use to borrow a book called ABC of Communism from writer Satyabhakta to teach socialism to his cadres.*

## Activities in Jhansi

*Azad made Jhansi his organization's hub for some time. He used the forest of Orchha, situated 15 kilometres (9.3 mi) from Jhansi, as a site for shooting practice and, being an expert marksman, he trained other members of his group. He built a hut near to a Hanuman temple on the banks of the Satar River and lived there under the alias of Pandit Harishankar Bramhachari for a long period. He taught children from the nearby village of Dhimarpura and thus managed to establish a good rapport with the local residents.*

*While living in Jhansi, he also learned to drive a car at the Bundelkhand Motor Garage in Sadar Bazar. Sadashivrao Malkapurkar, Vishwanath Vaishampayan and Bhagwan Das Mahaur came in close contact with him and became an integral part of his revolutionary group. The then congress leaders, Raghunath Vinayak Dhulekar and Sitaram Bhaskar Bhagwat were also close to Azad. He also stayed for some time in the house of Rudra Narayan Singh at Nai Basti, as well as Bhagwat's house in Nagra.*

## With Bhagat Singh

*The Hindustan Republican Association (HRA) was formed by Ram Prasad Bismil, Jogesh Chandra Chatterjee, Sachindra Nath Sanyal and Sachindra Nath Bakshi in 1923. In the aftermath of the Kakori train robbery in 1925, the British suppressed revolutionary activities. Prasad, Ashfaqulla Khan, Thakur Roshan Singh and Rajendra Nath Lahiri were sentenced to death for their participation. Azad, Keshab Chakravarthy and Murari Lal Gupta evaded capture. Azad later reorganized the HRA with the help of fellow revolutionaries like Shiv Verma and Mahabir Singh.*

*In 1928, along with Bhagat Singh and other revolutionaries he secretly reorganised the Hindustan Republican Association (HRA), renaming it as the Hindustan Socialist Republican Association (HSRA) on 8—9 September, so as to achieve their primary aim of an independent socialist India. Azad then conspired with revolutionaries like Shivaram Rajguru, Sukhdev Thapar, and Bhagat Singh to assassinate the Superintendent of police, James A. Scott in order to avenge Lala Rajpat Rai's death. However, in a case of mistaken identity, the plotters shot John P. Saunders, an Assistant Superintendent of Police, Azad shot dead an Indian police head constable Channan Singh, who attempted to give chase as Singh and Rajguru fled., as he was leaving the District Police Headquarters in Lahore on 17 December 1928. The insight of his revolutionary activities is described by Manmath Nath Gupta, a fellow member of HSRA in his numerous writings. Gupta has also written his biography titled "Chandrashekhar Azad" in his book History of the Indian Revolutionary Movement he gave a deep insight into Azad's activities, his ideologies, and the HSRA.*

## Death

*On 27 February 1931, the CID head of the police at Allahabad, J. R. H. Nott-Bower was tipped off by someone that Azad was at Alfred Park and was having a talk with his companion and aide Sukhdev Raj. On receiving it, Bower called on the Allahabad Police to accompany him to the park to arrest him. The police arrived at the park and surrounded it from all four sides. Some constables along with DSP Thakur Vishweshwar Singh entered the park armed with rifles and the shootout began. Azad killed three policemen but was badly wounded in the process of defending himself and helping his colleague Raj. Azad told him to move out in order to continue the freedom struggle and gave him cover fire for Raj to safely escape from the park. Azad hid behind a tree to save himself and began to fire from behind it. The police fired back. After a long shootout, holding true to his pledge to always remain Azad (Free) and never be captured alive, he shot himself in the head with his gun's last bullet. In the shootout, Bower and DSP Singh were injured in the right hand and jaws respectively. The police recovered Azad's body after the other officers arrived at the site. They were hesitant to come close to Azad after finding him dead.*

*The body was sent to Rasulabad Ghat for cremation without informing the general public. As it came to light, people surrounded the park where the incident had taken place. They chanted slogans against the British government and praised Azad.*

# CHAPTER FOUR

# KHUDIRAM BOSE

**Summary:**

*Khudiram Bose was an Indian nationalist from Bengal Presidency who opposed British rule of India. For his role in the Muzaffarpur Conspiracy Case, along with Prafulla Chaki, he was sentenced to Khudiram, along with Prafulla Chaki, attempted to assassinate a British judge, Magistrate Douglas Kingsford, by throwing bombs on the carriage they suspected the man was in. Magistrate Kingsford, however, was seated in a different carriage, and the throwing of bombs resulted in the deaths of two British women. Prafulla fatally shot himself before the arrest. Khudiram was arrested and trialed for the murder of the two women, ultimately being sentenced to death. He was one of the first Indian revolutionaries in Bengal to be executed by the British.*

KHUDIRAM BOSE

## Life Before Revolution

*Khudiram Bose was born on 3 December 1889 in a Bengali Kayastha family in the small village named Mohobani, situated under the Keshpur Police Station in the undivided Medinipur district of Bengal. His father was a Tehsildar in the Nerajol.*

*Khudiram was the fourth child in a family of three daughters. His parents, Trailokyanath Bose and Lakshmipriya Devi had two sons before the birth of Khudiram but both of them died prematurely. Following the traditional customs prevalent in the culture, the newborn child was symbolically sold to his eldest sister in exchange of three handfuls of food grains locally known as Khud, in an attempt to save him from dying at an early age. This way he acquired the name, Khudiram.*

*He lost his mother when he was Five years old. His father died a year after. Aparupa Roy, his elder sister, brought him to her house at Hatgachha village under the Daspur Police Station. Anurupadevi's husband, Amritalal Roy, got him admitted to Tamluk's Hamilton High School.*

*In 1902 and 1903, Sri Aurobindo and Sister Nivedita visited Midnapore. They held a series of public lectures and private session with the existing revolutionary groups for freedom. Khudiram, a teenager, was an active participant in the discussions about the revolution.*

*Apparently, he joined Anushilan Samiti, and came into contact with the network of Barindra Kumar Ghosh of Calcutta. He became a volunteer at the age of 15, and was arrested for distributing pamphlets against the British rule in India. At the young age of 16, Khudiram took part in planting bombs near the police stations and targeted government officials.*

## Kingsford Assassination Attempts

*The first attempt to kill Kingsford was in the form of a book bomb constructed by Hemchandra Kanungo, a revolutionary, who learnt bomb making techniques from Europe. An empty tin of Cadbury cocoa was packed with a pound of picric acid and three detonators. This was packed into a hollowed section of Herbert Broom's Commentaries on the Common Law and delivered wrapped in a brown paper to Kingsford's house by Paresh Mallick, a young revolutionary. Kingsford placed the unopened package in his shelf to examine later. By March 1908, fearful of the judge's safety, he was promoted to the District Judge position and transferred by the government to Muzaffarpur, Bihar. With him went his furniture, library and the book bomb.*

## The Reconnaissance at Muzaffarpur

*Anushilan Samiti persisted in their attempt to kill Kingsford. In April, a two-man reconnaissance team visited Muzaffarpur, which included Prafulla Chaki.[17] On their return, Hemchandra provided the bomb, which was composed of 6 ounces of dynamite, a detonator, and a black powder fuse. Prafulla Chaki returned to Muzaffarpur with a new boy, Khudiram Bose.*

## Police Suspicion

*The activities of Aurobindo Ghosh, Barindra Ghosh and their associates roused suspicion. The Calcutta police became aware of the plans on Kingsford's life. Commissioner F.L. Halliday's alerts to the Superintendent of Police in Muzzafarpur were ignored. However, four men were assigned to guard the magistrate's house. In the meantime, Khudiram Bose and Prafulla Chaki adopted the name of Haren Sarkar and Dinesh Chandra Roy respectively and took up residence in a charitable inn (Dharamshala) run by Kishorimohan Bandyopadhyay. In the ensuing days, the duo monitored the activities and daily routine of their target. The two revolutionaries successfully hid their identities for over three weeks. The CID officer from Calcutta returned with a letter from the Superintendent of Muzaffarpur, Armstrong, that the duo had not arrived. On the evening of 29 April, Khudiram and Prafulla were in place to execute their plans. Pretending to be schoolboys, they surveyed the Muzaffarpur park situated opposite The British Club, frequented by Kingsford. They were noticed by a constable.*

## Assassination attempts at Muzaffarpur

*On a fateful day, Kingsford and his wife were playing bridge with the daughter and wife of Pringle Kennedy, a British barrister. They decided to head home around 8.30 PM. Kingsford and his wife were in a carriage identical to the one carrying Kennedy and his family as their carriage reached the eastern gate of the compound of the European Club, Khudiram and Prafulla ran towards the carriage and threw the bombs into the carriage. A loud explosion ensued and the carriage was taken to Kingsford's house. The carriage was shattered and the Kennedy ladies sustained terrible injuries. Miss Kennedy died within an hour and Mrs. Kennedy died on 2 May of sustained injuries.*

## Escape

*Khudiram and Prafulla went their own way to escape capture. By morning, Khudiram had walked 25 miles and he reached a station called Waini. As he asked for a glass of water at a tea stall, he was confronted by two armed constables, Fateh Singh, and Sheo Pershad Singh, who immediately suspected something upon seeing his dusty feet, and his exhausted and perspiring appearance. After a couple of questions, their suspicion became stronger, and they decided to detain Khudiram. Khudiram started struggling with the two men, and immediately, one of the two hidden revolvers fell out. Before Khudiram could use the other one to fire on the constables, one of them held him from behind in a bear-hug. The much younger and lightly built Khudiram had no more chance of defence or escape. On his person were found 37 rounds of ammunition, Rs. 30 in cash, a railway map and a page of the rail timetable. The fate of Khudiram was sealed forever. The Waini station is now known as Khudiram Bose Pusa Station. On the other hand, Prafulla had travelled long arduous hours. Around midday, a civil named Trigunacharan Ghosh noticed a young way coming his way. He was aware of the bomb blast and realized that Prafulla was the other revolutionary. Ghosh decided to save his life, and let him bathe, eat, and rest in his house.[citation needed] He arranged for Prafulla to return to Kolkata the same night. He boarded a train from Samastipur for Mokamaghat, and continue his onward journey with a train to Howrah. A sub-inspector in the Indian Imperial Police, Nandalal Bannerjee, was travelling in the same compartment. He struck a conversation and realized Prafulla to be the other revolutionary. When Prafulla got down at the Shipwright station to drink water, Bannerjee sent a telegram to the Muzaffarpur police station. Banerjee tried to apprehend Prafulla at the Mokamaghat station. Prafulla tried to fight his way through with his revolver but in the end, down to his last bullet, he shot himself in the mouth. On 1 May, the handcuffed Khudiram was brought from to Muzaffarpur. The entire town descended at the police station to take a look at the teenage boy surrounded by a team of armed policemen. Khudiram was taken to the house of the district magistrate, Mr. Woodman. The English daily, The Statesman, wrote on the following day, 2 May 1908. The Railway station was crowded to see the boy. A mere boy of 18 or 19 years old, who looked quite determined. He came out of a first-class compartment and walked all the way to the phaeton, kept for him outside, like a cheerful boy who knows no anxiety.....on taking his seat the boy cheerfully cried 'Vandemataram'. Khudiram had to give a statement or declaration to the magistrate. He took full responsibility for the assassination, unknown that Prafulla was dead. Only after Khudiram finished giving his statement, the body of Prafulla reached Muzaffarpur. Khudiram realized that lying would go in vain. He identified the body of Prafulla and the British also received details from the encounter with sub-inspector Bannerjee. Instead of believing Khudiram, the British colonial authorities thought it more proper to detach Prafulla's head from his corpse and send it to Calcutta for better confirmation.*

## First hearing

*The historical trial started on 21 May 1908, presided by Judge Corndoff, Nathuni Prasad and Janak Prasad in the Jury. Along with Khudiram, two others were tried for assisting the revolutionaries in their mission — Mrityunjay Chakraborty and Kishorimohan Bandopadhyay, who had accommodated Khudiram Bose and Prafulla Chaki in his Dharmashala for their mission. Mrityunjay died during the trial, and subsequently, the trial of Kishorimohan was separated from that of Khudiram. Mannum and Binod Bihari Majumdar were the prosecutors for the British colonial government. Lawyers Kalidas Basu, Upendranath Sen, and Kshetranath Bandopadhyay took up Khudiram's defence. They were joined later in the trial by Kulkamal Sen, Nagendra Lal Lahiri, and Satischandra Chakraborty—all of them fought the case without any fees. On 23 May, Khudiram resubmitted his statement to magistrate E.W. Bredhowd, denying any involvement or responsibility in any aspect or stage of the entire mission and operation down to the bombing. Initially, Khudiram was not ready to sign this statement but did so after persuasion from his lawyers. On 13 June, the scheduled date for the verdict and sentence, the judge and the prosecutors received an anonymous letter of warning, which told them that there was one more bomb coming for them from Kolkata and that henceforth it will be the Biharis, and not the Bengalis, who are going to kill them. On the other hand, it made the defence lawyers more confident as the letter was proof there could be other masterminds and executors of the Muzaffarpur bombing other than Khudiram, and that along with Khudiram's age should make the judge deliver sentencing other than death. But, to the disappointment to all, the Judge pronounced the death sentence for Khudiram. Khudiram's immediate and spontaneous response was to smile. The judge, surprised, asked Khudiram whether he had understood the meaning of the pronounced sentence. Khudiram replied that he surely had. When the judge asked him again whether he had anything to say, in front of a packed audience, Khudiram replied with the same smile that if he could be given some time, he could teach the judge the skill of bomb-making. By then, the Judge was instructing the police to escort the boy out of the courtroom. As per the legal system, Khudiram had 7 days to appeal to the High Court. Khudiram refused to appeal. However, after some persuasion by his counselors — with the logic that if he receives a life sentence instead of getting hanged because of this appeal, he would live to serve his nation once free and he would have age on his side when that happens — Khudiram finally agreed, in a detached manner, to go along with his defence team.*

## Second hearing

*The High Court hearing took place on 8 July 1908. Narendrakumar Basu came to Khudiram's defence and concentrated all his legal skills and experience in this case to save a boy who had overnight become a wonder and a hero for the whole country. He challenged the verdict of the session court by saying that the judging was not according to law and was flawed. He reasoned that according to article 164 of the penal code, the accused is required to submit his statement in front of a first class magistrate, which Mr. Woodman was not, and moreover, during the first statement Khudiram was not told anything of the person's identity and position. Secondly, pointed out Basu, the article 364 requires that all questions to the accused be made in the mother tongue of the same, and all answers from the accused in his mother tongue be documented verbatim in that language, but which was done in English in Khudiram's case. Moreover, Khudiram's signature was required to be given on the statement on the same date and at the time of the statement in the presence of the magistrate, but in reality, Khudiram was made to sign the day after, and in front of a different person, who was an additional magistrate. Lastly, since such a statement is by definition required to be totally voluntary, with the magistrate being sure that it was so, there was no proof that Khudiram was allowed to give a voluntary statement without any direct or indirect manipulation after his capture. Lastly, Narendrakumar Basu said that Prafulla aka "Dinesh" (the name used in the trial) was stronger than Khudiram was, and he was the bomb-expert among the two of them. Thus, it is highly likely that the actual thrower of the bomb was "Dinesh". Further, Prafulla's suicide on the verge of capture only reinforces the possibility of his being the actual thrower of the bombs. After the defence, it was announced by the two British judges that the final verdict would be passed on 13 July 1908.*

## Judgement

*As Khudiram was the only of the two alive, his lone statement of a two-man team was the foundation for the entire case. Since all the legal arguments put forth by Narendrakumar Basu were believed to be technically correct, it was hoped that for the sake of the law—about which the British prided themselves ad infinitum — Khudiram's life would, at least, be spared. But, on a historical day, the British judges confirmed the conviction and sentence and dismissed the appeal.*

## Execution

*On 11 August, the region around the prison became packed with a swelling crowd before the scheduled time, 6 AM. People holding flower garlands filled up the front rows of the crowd. Upendranath Sen, the lawyer-journalist of the Bengali news daily "Bengalee", who was close to Khudiram, reports having reached the venue by 5 AM, in a car with all the necessary funerary arrangements and clothes. After the hanging, the funeral procession went through the city, with police guards holding back the crowd all along the central artery street. The people kept throwing their flowers on the body as the carriage passed by.*

*The Amrita Bazar Patrika, one of the prominent dailies of that era, carried the story of the hanging the next day, on 12 August. Under the headline "Khudiram's End: Died cheerful and smiling" the newspaper wrote:*

*"Khudiram's execution took place at 6 a.m. this morning. He walked to the gallows firmly and cheerfully and even smiled when the cap was drawn over his head."*

*An established Anglo-Indian newspaper, The Empire, wrote:*

*"Khudiram Bose was executed this morning...It is alleged that he mounted the scaffold with his body erect. He was cheerful and smiling."*

• 65 •

# CHAPTER FIVE

# SARDAR VALLABHBHAI PATEL

**Summary:**

*Sardar Vallabhbhai Patel, was an Indian independence activist and barrister who served as the first Deputy Prime Minister and Home Minister of India from 1947 to 1950. He was a senior leader of the Indian National Congress, who played a significant role in the Indian independence movement and India's political integration. In India and elsewhere, he was often called Sardar, meaning "Chief" in Hindi, Urdu, Bengali and Persian. He acted as the Home Minister during the political integration of India and the Indo-Pakistani War of 1947.*

SARDAR VALLABHBHAI PATEL

## Background

*Vallabhbhai Jhaverbhai Patel, one of the six children of Jhaverbhai Patel and Ladba, was born in Nadiad, Gujarat. He followed Vaishnavism and belonged to Pushtimarg sect of Mahaprabhu Vallabhacharya and took the diksha from the descendant of Vallabhacharya. Patel's date of birth was never officially recorded; Patel entered it as 31 October on his matriculation examination papers. He belonged to the Patidars, specifically the Leva Patel community of Central Gujarat; although after his fame, both Leva Patel and Kadava Patidar have claimed him as one of their own.*

*Patel travelled to attend schools in Nadiad, Petlad, and Borsad, living self-sufficiently with other boys. He reputedly cultivated a stoic character. A popular anecdote recounts that he lanced his own painful boil without hesitation, even as the barber charged with doing it trembled. When Patel passed his matriculation at the relatively late age of 22, he was generally regarded by his elders as an unambitious man destined for a commonplace job. Patel himself, though, harboured a plan to study to become a lawyer, work and save funds, travel to England, and become a barrister. Patel spent years away from his family, studying on his own with books borrowed from other lawyers, passing his examinations within two years. Fetching his wife Jhaverba from her parents' home, Patel set up his household in Godhra and was called to the bar. During the many years it took him to save money, Patel – now an advocate – earned a reputation as a fierce and skilled lawyer. The couple had a daughter, Maniben, in 1903 and a son, Dahyabhai, in 1905. Patel also cared for a friend suffering from the Bubonic plague when it swept across Gujarat. When Patel himself came down with the disease, he immediately sent his family to safety, left his home, and moved into an isolated house in Nadiad (by other accounts, Patel spent this time in a dilapidated temple).*

*Patel practised law in Godhra, Borsad, and Anand while taking on the financial burdens of his homestead in Karamsad. Patel was the first chairman and founder of "Edward Memorial High School" Borsad, today known as Jhaverbhai Dajibhai Patel High School. When he had saved enough for his trip to England and applied for a pass and a ticket, they were addressed to "V. J. Patel," at the home of his elder brother Vithalbhai, who had the same initials as Vallabhai. Having once nurtured a similar hope to study in England, Vithalbhai remonstrated his younger brother, saying that it would be disreputable for an older brother to follow his younger brother. In keeping with concerns for his family's honour, Patel allowed Vithalbhai to go in his place.*

*In 1909 Patel's wife Jhaverba was hospitalised in Bombay (present-day Mumbai) to undergo major surgery for cancer. Her health suddenly worsened and, despite successful emergency surgery, she died in the hospital. Patel was given a note informing him of his wife's demise as he was cross-examining a witness in court. According to witnesses, Patel read the note, pocketed it, and continued his cross-examination and won the case. He broke the news to others only after the proceedings had ended. Patel decided against marrying again. He raised his children with the help of his family and sent them to English-language schools in Bombay. At the age of 36, he journeyed to England and enrolled at the Middle Temple in London. Completing a 36-month course in 30 months, Patel finished at the top of his class despite having had no previous college background.*

*Returning to India, Patel settled in Ahmedabad and became one of the city's most successful barristers. Wearing European-style clothes and sporting urbane mannerisms, he became a skilled bridge player. In a TED talk on the game of Bridge, 12-year old World Bridge Champion Anshul Bhatt talks about the legendary lifelong partnership between Mahatma Gandhi and Sardar Patel built on the Bridge table while in prison. Patel nurtured ambitions to expand his practice and accumulate great wealth and to provide his children with modern education. He had made a pact with his brother Vithalbhai to support his entry into politics in the Bombay Presidency, while Patel remained in Ahmedabad to provide for the family.*

**Fight for Independence**

*In September 1917, Patel delivered a speech in Borsad, encouraging Indians nationwide to sign Gandhi's petition demanding Swaraj – self-rule –*

*from Britain. A month later, he met Gandhi for the first time at the Gujarat Political Conference in Godhra. On Gandhi's encouragement, Patel became the secretary of the Gujarat Sabha, a public body that would become the Gujarati arm of the Indian National Congress. Patel now energetically fought against veth – the forced servitude of Indians to Europeans – and organised relief efforts in the wake of plague and famine in Kheda. The Kheda peasants' plea for exemption from taxation had been turned down by British authorities. Gandhi endorsed waging a struggle there, but could not lead it himself due to his activities in Champaran. When Gandhi asked for a Gujarati activist to devote himself completely to the assignment, Patel volunteered, much to Gandhi's delight. Though his decision was made on the spot, Patel later said that his desire and commitment came after intense personal contemplation, as he realised he would have to abandon his career and material ambitions.*

## Satyagraha in Gujarat

*Patel, supported by Congress volunteers Narhari Parikh, Mohanlal Pandya, and Abbas Tyabji, Vallabhbhai Patel began a village-by-village tour in the Kheda district, documenting grievances and asking villagers for their support for a statewide revolt by refusing to pay taxes. Patel emphasised the potential hardships and the need for complete unity and non-violence in the face of provocation response from virtually every village. When the revolt was launched and tax revenue withheld, the government sent police and intimidation squads to seize property, including confiscating barn animals and whole farms. Patel organised a network of volunteers to work with individual villages, helping them hide valuables and protect themselves against raids. Thousands of activists and farmers were arrested, but Patel was not. The revolt evoked sympathy and admiration across India, including among pro-British Indian politicians. The government agreed to negotiate with Patel and decided to suspend the payment of taxes for a year, even scaling back the rate. Patel emerged as a hero to Gujaratis. In 1920 he was elected president of the newly formed Gujarat Pradesh Congress Committee; he would serve as its president until 1945.*

*Patel supported Gandhi's Non-cooperation movement and toured the state to recruit more than 300,000 members and raise over Rs. 1.5 million in funds. Helping organise bonfires in Ahmedabad in which British goods were burned, Patel threw in all his English-style clothes. Along with his daughter Mani and son Dahya, he switched completely to wearing khadi, the locally produced cotton clothing. Patel also supported Gandhi's controversial suspension of resistance in the wake of the Chauri Chaura incident. In Gujarat, he worked extensively in the following years against alcoholism, untouchability, and caste discrimination, as well as for the empowerment of women. In the Congress, he was a resolute supporter of Gandhi against his Swarajist critics. Patel was elected Ahmedabad's municipal president in 1922, 1924, and 1927. During his terms, he oversaw improvements in infrastructure: the supply of electricity was increased, drainage and sanitation systems were extended throughout the city. The school system underwent major reforms. He fought for the recognition and payment of teachers employed in schools established by nationalists (independent of British control) and even took on sensitive Hindu–Muslim issues. Patel personally led relief efforts in the aftermath of the torrential rainfall of 1927 that caused major floods in the city and in the Kheda district, and great destruction of life and property. He established refugee centres across the district, mobilised volunteers, and arranged for supplies of food, medicines, and clothing, as well as emergency funds from the government and the public.*

*When Gandhi was in prison, Patel was asked by Members of Congress to lead the satyagraha in Nagpur in 1923 against a law banning the raising of the Indian flag. He organised thousands of volunteers from all over the country to take part in processions of people violating the law. Patel negotiated a settlement obtaining the release of all prisoners and allowing nationalists to hoist the flag in public. Later that year, Patel and his allies uncovered evidence suggesting that the police were in league with a local dacoit/ criminal gang-related to Devar Baba in the Borsad taluka even as the government prepared to levy a major tax for fighting dacoits in the area. More than 6,000 villagers assembled to hear Patel speak in support of proposed agitation against the tax, which was deemed immoral and unnecessary. He organised hundreds of Congressmen, sent instructions, and received information from across the district. Every village in the taluka resisted payment of the tax and prevented the seizure of property and land. After a protracted struggle, the government withdrew the tax. Historians believe that one of Patel's key achievements was the building of cohesion and trust amongst the different castes and communities, which had been divided along socio-economic lines.*

*In April 1928 Patel returned to the independence struggle from his municipal duties in Ahmedabad when Bardoli suffered from a serious double predicament of a famine and a steep tax hike. The revenue hike was steeper than it had been in Kheda even though the famine covered a large portion of Gujarat. After cross-examining and talking to village representatives, emphasising the potential hardship and need for non-violence and cohesion, Patel initiated the struggle with a complete denial of taxes. Patel organised volunteers, camps, and an information network across affected areas. The revenue refusal was stronger than in Kheda, and many sympathy satyagrahas were undertaken across Gujarat. Despite arrests and seizures of property and land, the struggle intensified. The situation came to a head in August, when, through sympathetic intermediaries, he negotiated a settlement that included repealing the tax hike, reinstating village officials who had resigned in protest, and returning seized property and land. It was by the women of Bardoli, during the struggle and after the Indian National Congress victory in that area, that Patel first began to be referred to as Sardar (or chief).*

# Fundamental Rights and Economic Policy: 1931

*Under the chairmanship of Sardar Patel "Fundamental Rights and Economic Policy" resolution was passed by the Congress in 1931. As Gandhi embarked on the Dandi Salt March, Patel was arrested in the village of Ras and was put on trial without witnesses, with no lawyer or journalists allowed to attend. Patel's arrest and Gandhi's subsequent arrest caused the Salt Satyagraha to greatly intensify in Gujarat – districts across Gujarat launched an anti-tax rebellion until and unless Patel and Gandhi were released. Once released, Patel served as interim Congress president, but was re-arrested while leading a procession in Bombay. After the signing of the Gandhi–Irwin Pact, Patel was elected president of Congress for its 1931 session in Karachi – here the Congress ratified the pact and committed itself to the defence of fundamental rights and civil liberties. It advocated the establishment of a secular nation with a minimum wage and the abolition of untouchability and serfdom. Patel used his position as Congress president to organise the return of confiscated land to farmers in Gujarat. Upon the failure of the Round Table Conference in London, Gandhi and Patel were arrested in January 1932 when the struggle re-opened, and imprisoned in the Yeravda Central Jail. During this term of imprisonment, Patel and Gandhi grew close to each other, and the two developed a close bond of affection, trust, and frankness. Their mutual relationship could be described as that of an elder brother (Gandhi) and his younger brother (Patel). Despite having arguments with Gandhi, Patel respected his instincts and leadership. In prison, the two discussed national and social issues, read Hindu epics, and cracked jokes. Gandhi taught Patel Sanskrit. Gandhi's secretary, Mahadev Desai, kept detailed records of conversations between Gandhi and Patel. When Gandhi embarked on a fast-unto-death protesting the separate electorates allocated for untouchables, Patel looked after Gandhi closely and himself refrained from partaking of food. Patel was later moved to a jail in Nasik, and refused a British offer for a brief release to attend the cremation of his brother Vithalbhai, who had died in October 1933. He was finally released in July 1934.*

*Patel's position at the highest level in the Congress was largely connected with his role from 1934 onwards (when the Congress abandoned its boycott of elections) in the party organisation. Based at an apartment in Bombay, he became the Congress's main fundraiser and chairman of its Central Parliamentary Board, playing the leading role in selecting and financing candidates for the 1934 elections to the Central Legislative Assembly in New Delhi and for the provincial elections of 1936. In addition to collecting funds and selecting candidates, he also determined the Congress's stance on issues and opponents. Not contesting a seat for himself, Patel nevertheless guided Congressmen elected in the provinces and at the national level. In 1935 Patel underwent surgery for haemorrhoids, yet continued to direct efforts against the plague in Bardoli and again when a drought struck Gujarat in 1939. Patel guided the Congress ministries that had won power across India with the aim of preserving party discipline – Patel feared that the British government would take advantage of opportunities to create conflict among elected Congressmen, and he did not want the party to be distracted from the goal of complete independence. Patel clashed with Nehru, opposing declarations of the adoption of socialism at the 1936 Congress session, which he believed was a diversion from the main goal of achieving independence. In 1938 Patel organised rank and file opposition to the attempts of then-Congress president Subhas Chandra Bose to move away from Gandhi's principles of non-violent resistance. Patel saw Bose as wanting more power over the party. He led senior Congress leaders in a protest that resulted in Bose's resignation. But criticism arose from Bose's supporters, socialists, and other Congressmen that Patel himself was acting in an authoritarian manner in his defence of Gandhi's authority.*

## Legal Battle with Subhas Chandra Bose

*Vithalbhai and Bose had been highly critical of Gandhi's leadership during their travels in Europe. "By the time Vithalbhai died in October 1933, Bose had become his primary caregiver. On his deathbed he left a will of sorts, bequeathing three-quarters of his money to Bose to use in promoting India's cause in other countries. When Patel saw a copy of the letter in which his brother had left a majority of his estate to Bose, he asked a series of questions: Why was the letter not attested by a doctor? Had the original paper been preserved? Why were the witnesses to that letter all men from Bengal and none of the many other veteran freedom activists and supporters of the Congress who had been present at Geneva where Vithalbhai had died? Patel may even have doubted the veracity of the signature on the document. The case went to the court and after a legal battle that lasted more than a year, the courts judged that Vithalbhai's estate could only be inherited by his legal heirs, that is, his family. Patel promptly handed the money over to the Vithalbhai Memorial Trust."*

## Quit India Movement

*On the outbreak of World War II, Patel supported Nehru's decision to withdraw the Congress from central and provincial legislatures, contrary to Gandhi's advice, as well as an initiative by senior leader Chakravarthi Rajagopalachari to offer Congress's full support to Britain if it promised Indian independence at the end of the war and installed a democratic government right away. Gandhi had refused to support Britain on the grounds of his moral opposition to war, while Subhash Chandra Bose was in militant opposition to the British. The British government rejected Rajagopalachari's initiative, and Patel embraced Gandhi's leadership again. He participated in Gandhi's call for individual disobedience, and was arrested in 1940 and imprisoned for nine months. He also opposed the proposals of the Cripps' mission in 1942. Patel lost more than twenty pounds during his period in jail.*

*While Nehru, Rajagopalachari, and Maulana Azad initially criticised Gandhi's proposal for an all-out campaign of civil disobedience to force the British to grant Indian independence, Patel was its most fervent supporter. Arguing that the British would retreat from India as they had from Singapore and Burma, Patel urged that the campaign start without any delay. Though feeling that the British would not leave immediately, Patel favoured an all-out rebellion that would galvanise the Indian people, who had been divided in their response to the war. In Patel's view, such a rebellion would force the British to concede that continuation of colonial rule had no support in India, and thus speed the transfer of power to Indians. Believing strongly in the need for revolt, Patel stated his intention to resign from the Congress if the revolt were not approved. Gandhi strongly pressured the All India Congress Committee to approve an all-out campaign of civil disobedience, and the AICC approved the campaign on 7 August 1942. Though Patel's health had suffered during his stint in jail, he gave emotional speeches to large crowds across India, asking them to refuse to pay taxes and to participate in civil disobedience, mass protests, and a shutdown of all civil services. He raised funds and prepared a second tier of command as a precaution against the arrest of national leaders. Patel made a climactic speech to more than 100,000 people gathered at Gowalia Tank in Bombay on 7 August:*

*The Governor of Burma boasts in London that they left Burma only after reducing everything to dust. So you promise the same thing to India? ... You refer in your radio broadcasts and newspapers to the government established in Burma by Japan as a puppet government? What sort of government do you have in Delhi now?...When France fell before the Nazi onslaught, in the midst of total war, Mr. Churchill offered union with England to the French. That was indeed a stroke of inspired statesmanship. But when it comes to India? Oh no! Constitutional changes in the midst of a war? Absolutely unthinkable ... The objective this time is to free India before the Japanese can come and be ready to fight them if they come. They will round up the leaders, round up all. Then it will be the duty of every Indian to put forth his utmost effort—within non-violence. No source is to be left untapped; no weapon untried. This is going to be the opportunity of a lifetime.*

*Historians believe that Patel's speech was instrumental in electrifying nationalists, who up to then had been sceptical of the proposed rebellion. Patel's organising work in this period is credited by historians with ensuring the success of the rebellion across India. Patel was arrested on 9 August and was imprisoned with the entire Congress Working Committee from 1942 to 1945 at the fort in Ahmednagar. Here he spun cloth, played bridge, read a large number of books, took long walks, and practised gardening. He also provided emotional support to his colleagues while awaiting news and developments from the outside. Patel was deeply pained at the news of the deaths of Mahadev Desai and Kasturba Gandhi later that year. But Patel wrote in a letter to his daughter that he and his colleagues were experiencing "fullest peace" for having done "their duty". Even though other political parties had opposed the struggle and the British colonial government had responded by imprisoning most of the leaders of Congress, the Quit India movement was "by far the most serious rebellion since that of 1857", as the viceroy cabled to Winston Churchill. More than 100,000 people were arrested and numerous protestors were killed in violent confrontations with the Indian Imperial Police. Strikes, protests, and other revolutionary activities had broken out across India. When Patel was released on 15 June 1945, he realised that the British government was preparing proposals to transfer power to India.*

## Partition and independence

*In the 1946 Indian provincial elections, the Congress won a large majority of the elected seats, dominating the Hindu electorate. However the Muslim League led by Muhammad Ali Jinnah won a large majority of Muslim electorate seats. The League had resolved in 1940 to demand Pakistan – an independent state for Muslims – and was a fierce critic of the Congress. The Congress formed governments in all provinces save Sindh, Punjab, and Bengal, where it entered into coalitions with other parties.*

## Cabinet mission and partition

*When the British mission proposed two plans for transfer of power, there was considerable opposition within the Congress to both. The plan of 16 May 1946 proposed a loose federation with extensive provincial autonomy, and the "grouping" of provinces based on religious-majority. The plan of 16 May 1946 proposed the partition of India on religious lines, with over 565 princely states free to choose between independence or accession to either dominion. The League approved both plans while the Congress flatly rejected the proposal of 16 May. Gandhi criticised the 16 May proposal as being inherently divisive, but Patel, realising that rejecting the proposal would mean that only the League would be invited to form a government, lobbied the Congress Working Committee hard to give its assent to the 16 May proposal. Patel engaged in discussions with the British envoys Sir Stafford Cripps and Lord Pethick-Lawrence and obtained an assurance that the "grouping" clause would not be given practical force, Patel converted Jawaharlal Nehru, Rajendra Prasad, and Rajagopalachari to accept the plan. When the League retracted its approval of the 16 May plan, the viceroy Lord Wavell invited the Congress to form the government. Under Nehru, who was styled the "Vice President of the Viceroy's Executive Council", Patel took charge of the departments of home affairs and information and broadcasting. He moved into a government house on Aurangzeb Road in Delhi, which would be his home until his death in 1950.*

*Vallabhbhai Patel was one of the first Congress leaders to accept the partition of India as a solution to the rising Muslim separatist movement led by Muhammad Ali Jinnah. He had been outraged by Jinnah's Direct Action campaign, which had provoked communal violence across India, and by the viceroy's vetoes of his home department's plans to stop the violence on the grounds of constitutionality. Patel severely criticised the viceroy's induction of League ministers into the government, and the revalidation of the grouping scheme by the British government without Congress's approval. Although further outraged at the League's boycott of the assembly and non-acceptance of the plan of 16 May despite entering government, he was also aware that Jinnah did enjoy popular support amongst Muslims, and that an open conflict between him and the nationalists could degenerate into a Hindu-Muslim civil war of disastrous consequences. The continuation of a divided and weak central government would, in Patel's mind, result in the wider fragmentation of India by encouraging more than 600 princely states towards independence. In December 1946 and January 1947, Patel worked with civil servant V. P. Menon on the latter's suggestion for a separate dominion of Pakistan created out of Muslim-majority provinces. Communal violence in Bengal and Punjab in January and March 1947 further convinced Patel of the soundness of partition. Patel, a fierce critic of Jinnah's demand that the Hindu-majority areas of Punjab and Bengal be included in a Muslim state, obtained the partition of those provinces, thus blocking any possibility of their inclusion in Pakistan. Patel's decisiveness on the partition of Punjab and Bengal had won him many supporters and admirers amongst the Indian public, which had tired of the League's tactics, but he was criticised by Gandhi, Nehru, secular Muslims, and socialists for a perceived eagerness to do so. When Lord Louis Mountbatten formally proposed the plan on 3 June 1947, Patel gave his approval and lobbied Nehru and other Congress leaders to accept the proposal. Knowing Gandhi's deep anguish regarding proposals of partition, Patel engaged him in frank discussion in private meetings over what he saw as the practical unworkability of any Congress–League coalition, the rising violence, and the threat of civil war. At the All India Congress Committee meeting called to vote on the proposal, Patel said:*

**"I fully appreciate the fears of our brothers from [the Muslim-majority areas]. Nobody likes the division of India and my heart is heavy. But the choice is between one division and many divisions. We must face facts. We cannot give way to emotionalism and sentimentality. The Working Committee has not acted out of fear. But I am afraid of one thing, that all our toil and hard work of these many years might go waste or prove unfruitful. My nine months in office has completely disillusioned me regarding the supposed merits of the Cabinet Mission Plan. Except for a few honourable exceptions, Muslim officials from the top down to the chaprasis (peons or servants) are working for the League. The communal veto given to the League in the Mission Plan would have blocked India's progress at every stage. Whether we like it or not, de facto Pakistan already exists in the Punjab and Bengal. Under the circumstances I would prefer a de jure Pakistan, which may make the League more responsible. Freedom is coming. We have 75 to 80 percent of India, which we can make strong with our own genius. The League can develop the rest of the country."**

*After Gandhi rejected and Congress approved the plan, Patel represented India on the Partition Council, where he oversaw the division of public assets, and selected the Indian council of ministers with Nehru. However, neither Patel nor any other Indian leader had foreseen the intense violence and population transfer that would take place with partition. Patel took the lead in organising relief and emergency supplies, establishing refugee camps, and visiting the border areas with Pakistani leaders to encourage peace. Despite these efforts, the death toll is estimated at between 500,000 and 1 million people. The estimated number of refugees in both countries exceeds 15 million. Understanding that Delhi and Punjab policemen, accused of organising attacks on Muslims, were personally affected by the tragedies of partition, Patel called out the Indian Army with South Indian regiments to restore order, imposing strict curfews and shoot-on-sight orders. Visiting the Nizamuddin Auliya Dargah area in Delhi, where thousands of Delhi Muslims feared attacks, he prayed at the shrine, visited the people, and reinforced the presence of police. He suppressed from the press reports of atrocities in Pakistan against Hindus and Sikhs to prevent retaliatory violence. Establishing the Delhi Emergency Committee to restore order and organising relief efforts for refugees in the capital, Patel publicly warned officials against partiality and neglect. When reports reached Patel that large groups of Sikhs were preparing to attack Muslim convoys heading for Pakistan, Patel hurried to Amritsar and met Sikh and Hindu leaders. Arguing that attacking helpless people was cowardly and dishonourable, Patel emphasised that Sikh actions would result in further attacks against Hindus and Sikhs in Pakistan. He assured the community leaders that if they worked to establish peace and order and guarantee the safety of Muslims, the Indian government would react forcefully to any failures of Pakistan to do the same. Additionally, Patel addressed a massive crowd of approximately 200,000 refugees who had surrounded his car after the meetings:*

*Here, in this same city, the blood of Hindus, Sikhs and Muslims mingled in the bloodbath of Jallianwala Bagh. I am grieved to think that things have come to such a pass that no Muslim can go about in Amritsar and no Hindu or Sikh can even think of living in Lahore. The butchery of innocent and defenceless men, women and children does not behove brave men ... I am quite certain that India's interest lies in getting all her men and women across the border and sending out all Muslims from East Punjab. I have come to you with a specific appeal. Pledge the safety of Muslim refugees crossing the city. Any obstacles or hindrances will only worsen the plight of our refugees who are already performing prodigious feats of endurance. If we have to fight, we must fight clean. Such a fight must await an appropriate time and conditions and you must be watchful in choosing your ground. To fight against the refugees is no fight at all. No laws of humanity or war among honourable men permit the murder of people who have sought shelter and protection. Let there be truce for three months in which both sides can exchange their refugees. This sort of truce is permitted even by laws of war. Let us take the initiative in breaking this vicious circle of attacks and counter-attacks. Hold your hands for a week and see what happens. Make way for the refugees with your own force of volunteers and let them deliver the refugees safely at our frontier.*

*Following his dialogue with community leaders and his speech, no further attacks occurred against Muslim refugees, and a wider peace and order was soon re-established over the entire area. However, Patel was criticised by Nehru, secular Muslims, and Gandhi over his alleged wish to see Muslims from other parts of India depart. While Patel vehemently denied such allegations, the acrimony with Maulana Azad and other secular Muslim leaders increased when Patel refused to dismiss Delhi's Sikh police commissioner, who was accused of discrimination. Hindu and Sikh leaders also accused Patel and other leaders of not taking Pakistan sufficiently to task over the attacks on their communities there, and Muslim leaders further criticised him for allegedly neglecting the needs of Muslims leaving for Pakistan, and concentrating resources for incoming Hindu and Sikh refugees. Patel clashed with Nehru and Azad over the allocation of houses in Delhi vacated by Muslims leaving for Pakistan; Nehru and Azad desired to allocate them for displaced Muslims, while Patel argued that no government professing secularism must make such exclusions. However, Patel was publicly defended by Gandhi and received widespread admiration and support for speaking frankly on communal issues and acting decisively and resourcefully to quell disorder and violence.*

# Political integration of Independent India

*As the first Home Minister, Patel played one of the major role in the integration of the princely states into the Indian federation. This achievement formed the cornerstone of Patel's popularity in the post-independence era. He is, in this regard, compared to Otto von Bismarck who unified the many German states in 1871. Under the plan of 3 June, more than 565 princely states were given the option of joining either India or Pakistan, or choosing independence. Indian nationalists and large segments of the public feared that if these states did not accede, most of the people and territory would be fragmented. The Congress, as well as senior British officials, considered Patel the best man for the task of achieving conquest of the princely states by the Indian dominion. Gandhi had said to Patel, "The problem of the States is so difficult that you alone can solve it". Patel was considered a statesman of integrity with the practical acumen and resolve to accomplish a monumental task. He asked V. P. Menon, a senior civil servant with whom he had worked on the partition of India, to become his right-hand man as chief secretary of the States Ministry. On 6 August 1947, Patel began lobbying the princes, attempting to make them receptive towards dialogue with the future government and forestall potential conflicts. Patel used social meetings and unofficial surroundings to engage most of the monarchs, inviting them to lunch and tea at his home in Delhi. At these meetings, Patel explained that there was no inherent conflict between the Congress and the princely order. Patel invoked the patriotism of India's monarchs, asking them to join in the independence of their nation and act as responsible rulers who cared about the future of their people. He persuaded the princes of 565 states of the impossibility of independence from the Indian republic, especially in the presence of growing opposition from their subjects. He proposed favourable terms for the merger, including the creation of privy purses for the rulers' descendants. While encouraging the rulers to act out of patriotism, Patel did not rule out force. Stressing that the princes would need to accede to India in good faith, he set a deadline of 15 August 1947 for them to sign the instrument of accession document. All but three of the states willingly merged into the Indian union; only Jammu and Kashmir, Junagadh, and Hyderabad did not fall into his basket.*

## Somnath temple Restoration

*Patel ordered Somnath temple reconstructed in 1948.*

*Hyderabad state in 1909. Its area stretched over large parts of the current Indian states of Telangana, Karnataka, and Maharashtra.*

## The British Indian Empire in 1909

*Junagadh was especially important to Patel, since it was in his home state of Gujarat. It was also important because in this Kathiawar district was the ultra-rich Somnath temple (which in the 11ᵗʰ century had been plundered by Mahmud of Ghazni, who damaged the temple and its idols to rob it of its riches, including emeralds, diamonds, and gold). Under pressure from Sir Shah Nawaz Bhutto, the Nawab had acceded to Pakistan. It was, however, quite far from Pakistan, and 80% of its population was Hindu. Patel combined diplomacy with force, demanding that Pakistan annul the accession, and that the Nawab accede to India. He sent the Army to occupy three principalities of Junagadh to show his resolve. Following widespread protests and the formation of a civil government, or Aarzi Hukumat, both Bhutto and the Nawab fled to Karachi, and under Patel's orders the Indian Army and police units marched into the state. A plebiscite organised later produced a 99.5% vote for merger with India.[68] In a speech at the Bahauddin College in Junagadh following the latter's take-over, Patel emphasised his feeling of urgency on Hyderabad, which he felt was more vital to India than Kashmir:*

*If Hyderabad does not see the writing on the wall, it goes the way Junagadh has gone. Pakistan attempted to set off Kashmir against Junagadh. When we raised the question of settlement in a democratic way, they (Pakistan) at once told us that they would consider it if we applied that policy to Kashmir. Our reply was that we would agree to Kashmir if they agreed to Hyderabad.*

*Hyderabad was the largest of the princely states, and it included parts of present-day Telangana, Andhra*

*Pradesh, Karnataka, and Maharashtra states. Its ruler, the Nizam Osman Ali Khan, was a Muslim, although over 80% of its people were Hindu. The Nizam sought independence or accession with Pakistan. Muslim forces loyal to Nizam, called the Razakars, under Qasim Razvi, pressed the Nizam to hold out against India, while organising attacks on people on Indian soil. Even though a Standstill Agreement was signed due to the desperate efforts of Lord Mountbatten to avoid a war, the Nizam rejected deals and changed his positions. On September 7, Jawaharlal Nehru gave ultimatum to Nizam, demanding ban on the Razakars and return of Indian troops to Secunderabad. Pakistan foreign minister Muhammad Zafarullah Khan warned India against this ultimatum. The invasion of Hyderabad was then launched on 13 September, after the death of Jinnah on 11 September." After the defeat of Razakars, the Nizam signed an instrument of accession, joining India.*

## Leading India

*The Governor-General of India, Chakravarti Rajagopalachari, along with Nehru and Patel, formed the "triumvirate" that ruled India from 1948 to 1950. Prime Minister Nehru was intensely popular with the masses, but Patel enjoyed the loyalty and the faith of rank and file Congressmen, state leaders, and India's civil servants. Patel was a senior leader in the Constituent Assembly of India and was responsible in large measure for shaping India's constitution.*

*Patel was the chairman of the committees responsible for minorities, tribal and excluded areas, fundamental rights, and provincial constitutions. Patel piloted a model constitution for the provinces in the Assembly, which contained limited powers for the state governor, who would defer to the president – he clarified it was not the intention to let the governor exercise power that could impede an elected government. He worked closely with Muslim leaders to end separate electorates and the more potent demand for reservation of seats for minorities. His intervention was key to the passage of two articles that protected civil servants from political involvement and guaranteed their terms and privileges. He was also instrumental in the founding the Indian Administrative Service and the Indian Police Service, and for his defence of Indian civil servants from political attack; he is known as the "patron saint" of India's services. When a delegation of Gujarati farmers came to him citing their inability to send their milk production to the markets without being fleeced by intermediaries, Patel exhorted them to organise the processing and sale of milk by themselves, and guided them to create the Kaira District Co-operative Milk Producers' Union Limited, which preceded the Amul milk products brand. Patel also pledged the reconstruction of the ancient but dilapidated Somnath Temple in Saurashtra. He oversaw the restoration work and the creation of a public trust, and pledged to dedicate the temple upon the completion of work (the work was completed after his death and the temple was inaugurated by the first President of India, Dr. Rajendra Prasad).*

*When the Pakistani invasion of Kashmir began in September 1947, Patel immediately wanted to send troops into Kashmir. But, agreeing with Nehru and Mountbatten, he waited until Kashmir's monarch had acceded to India. Patel then oversaw India's military operations to secure Srinagar and the Baramulla Pass, and the forces retrieved much territory from the invaders. Patel, along with Defence Minister Baldev Singh, administered the entire military effort, arranging for troops from different parts of India to be rushed to Kashmir and for a major military road connecting Srinagar to Pathankot to be built in six months. Patel strongly advised Nehru against going for arbitration to the United Nations, insisting that Pakistan had been wrong to support the invasion and the accession to India was valid. He did not want foreign interference in a bilateral affair. Patel opposed the release of Rs. 550 million to the Government of Pakistan, convinced that the money would go to finance the war against India in Kashmir. The Cabinet had approved his point but it was reversed when Gandhi, who feared an intensifying rivalry and further communal violence, went on a fast-unto-death to obtain the release. Patel, though not estranged from Gandhi, was deeply hurt at the rejection of his counsel and a Cabinet decision.*

*In 1949 a crisis arose when the number of Hindu refugees entering West Bengal, Assam, and Tripura from East Pakistan climbed to over 800,000. The refugees in many cases were being forcibly evicted by Pakistani authorities, and were victims of intimidation and violence. Nehru invited Liaquat Ali*

*Khan, Prime Minister of Pakistan, to find a peaceful solution. Despite his aversion, Patel reluctantly met Khan and discussed the matter. Patel strongly criticised Nehru's plan to sign a pact that would create minority commissions in both countries and pledge both India and Pakistan to a commitment to protect each other's minorities.[81] Syama Prasad Mookerjee and K. C. Neogy, two Bengali ministers, resigned, and Nehru was intensely criticised in West Bengal for allegedly appeasing Pakistan. The pact was immediately in jeopardy. Patel, however, publicly came to Nehru's aid. He gave emotional speeches to members of Parliament, and the people of West Bengal, and spoke with scores of delegations of Congressmen, Hindus, Muslims, and other public interest groups, persuading them to give peace a final effort.*

## Father of All India Services

*There is no alternative to this administrative system... The Union will go, you will not have a united India if you do not have good All-India Service which has the independence to speak out its mind, which has sense of security that you will standby your work... If you do not adopt this course, then do not follow the present Constitution. Substitute something else... these people are the instrument. Remove them and I see nothing but a picture of chaos all over the country.*

*He was also instrumental in the creation of the All India Services which he described as the country's*

*"Steel Frame". In his address to the probationers of these services, he asked them to be guided by the spirit of service in day-to-day administration. He reminded them that the ICS was no-longer neither Imperial, nor civil, nor imbued with any spirit of service after Independence. His exhortation to the probationers to maintain utmost impartiality and incorruptibility of administration is as relevant today as it was then. "A civil servant cannot afford to, and must not, take part in politics. Nor must he involve himself in communal wrangles. To depart from the path of rectitude in either of these respects is to debase public service and to lower its dignity," he had cautioned them on 21 April 1947.*

*He, more than anyone else in post-independence India, realised the crucial role that civil services play in administering a country, in not merely maintaining law and order, but running the institutions that provide the binding cement to a society. He, more than any other contemporary of his, was aware of the needs of a sound, stable administrative structure as the lynchpin of a functioning polity. The present-day all-India administrative services owe their origin to the man's sagacity and thus he is regarded as Father of modern All India Services.*

## Relations with Gandhi and Nehru

*Patel was intensely loyal to Gandhi, and both he and Nehru looked to him to arbitrate disputes. However, Nehru and Patel sparred over national issues. When*

*Nehru asserted control over Kashmir policy, Patel objected to Nehru's sidelining his home ministry's officials. Nehru was offended by Patel's decision-making regarding the states' integration, having consulted neither him nor the Cabinet. Patel asked Gandhi to relieve him of his obligation to serve, believing that an open political battle would hurt India. After much personal deliberation and contrary to Patel's prediction, Gandhi on 30 January 1948 told Patel not to leave the government. A free India, according to Gandhi, needed both Patel and Nehru. Patel was the last man to privately talk with Gandhi, who was assassinated just minutes after Patel's departure. At Gandhi's wake, Nehru and Patel embraced each other and addressed the nation together. Patel gave solace to many associates and friends and immediately moved to forestall any possible violence. Within two months of Gandhi's death, Patel suffered a major heart attack; the timely action of his daughter, his secretary, and a nurse saved Patel's life. Speaking later, Patel attributed the attack to the grief bottled up due to Gandhi's death.*

*Criticism arose from the media and other politicians that Patel's home ministry had failed to protect Gandhi. Emotionally exhausted, Patel tendered a letter of resignation, offering to leave the government. Patel's secretary persuaded him to withhold the letter, seeing it as fodder for Patel's political enemies and political conflict in India. However, Nehru sent Patel a letter dismissing any question of personal differences or desire for Patel's ouster. He reminded Patel of their 30-year partnership in the independence struggle and asserted that after Gandhi's death, it was especially wrong for them to quarrel. Nehru, Rajagopalachari, and other Congressmen publicly defended Patel. Moved, Patel publicly endorsed Nehru's leadership and refuted any suggestion of discord, and dispelled any notion that he sought to be prime minister.*

*Nehru gave Patel a free hand in integrating the princely states into India. Though the two committed themselves to joint leadership and non-interference in Congress party affairs, they sometimes would criticise each other in matters of policy, clashing on the issues of Hyderabad's integration and UN mediation in Kashmir. Nehru declined Patel's counsel on sending assistance to Tibet after its 1950 invasion by the People's Republic of China and on ejecting the Portuguese from Goa by military force.*

*When Nehru pressured Rajendra Prasad to decline a nomination to become the first President of India in 1950 in favour of Rajagopalachari, he angered the party, which felt Nehru was attempting to impose his will. Nehru sought Patel's help in winning the party over, but Patel declined, and Prasad was duly elected. Nehru opposed the 1950 Congress presidential candidate Purushottam Das Tandon, a conservative Hindu leader, endorsing Jivatram Kripalani instead and threatening to resign if Tandon was elected. Patel rejected Nehru's views and endorsed Tandon in Gujarat, where Kripalani received not one vote despite hailing from that state himself. Patel believed Nehru had to understand that his will was not law with the Congress, but he personally discouraged Nehru from resigning after the latter felt that the party had no confidence in him.*

## Ban on RSS

*The other is the R.S.S. I have made them an open offer. Change your plans, give up secrecy, respect the Constitution of India, show your loyalty to the (National Flag) and make us believe that we can trust your words. Whether they are friends or foes, and even if they are our own dear children, we are not going to allow them to play with fire so that the house may be set on fire. It would be criminal to allow young men to indulge in acts of violence and destruction..*

*In January 1948, Mahatma Gandhi was assassinated by Hindutva activist Nathuram Godse. Following the assassination, many prominent leaders of the Hindu nationalist organisation Rashtriya Swayamsevak Sangh (RSS) were arrested, and the organisation was banned on 4 February 1948 by Patel. During the court proceedings in relation to the assassination Godse began claiming that he had left the organisation in 1946.[101] Vallabhbhai Patel had remarked that the "RSS men expressed joy and distributed sweets after Gandhi's death".*

*The charged RSS leaders were acquitted of the conspiracy charge by the Supreme Court of India. Following his release in August 1948, Golwalkar wrote to Prime Minister Jawaharlal Nehru to lift the ban on RSS. After Nehru replied that the matter was the responsibility of the Home Minister, Golwalkar consulted Vallabhbhai Patel regarding the same. Patel then demanded an absolute pre-condition that the RSS adopt a formal written constitution and make it public, where Patel expected RSS to pledge its loyalty to the Constitution of India, accept the Tricolor as the National Flag of India, define the power of the head of the organisation, make the organisation democratic by holding internal elections, authorisation of their parents before enrolling the pre-adolescents into the movement, and to renounce violence and secrecy.*

*Golwalkar launched a huge agitation against this demand during which he was imprisoned again. Later, a constitution was drafted for RSS, which, however, initially did not meet any of Patel's demands. After a failed attempt to agitate again, eventually the RSS's constitution was amended according to Patel's wishes with the exception of the procedure for selecting the head of the organisation and the enrolment of pre-adolescents. However, the organisation's internal democracy which was written into its constitution, remained a 'dead letter'.*

*On 11 July 1949 the Government of India lifted the ban on the RSS by issuing a communique stating that the decision to lift the ban on the RSS had been taken in view of the RSS leader Golwalkar's undertaking to make the group's loyalty towards the Constitution of India and acceptance and respect towards the National Flag of India more explicit in the Constitution of the RSS, which was to be worked out in a democratic manner.*

## Final years

*In his twilight years, Patel was honoured by members of Parliament. He was awarded honorary doctorates of law by Nagpur University, the University of Allahabad and Banaras Hindu University in November 1948, subsequently receiving honorary doctorates from Osmania University in February 1949 and from Punjab University in March 1949. Previously, Patel had been featured on the cover page of the January 1947 issue of Time magazine.*

*On 29 March 1949 authorities lost radio contact with a Royal Indian Air Force de Havilland Dove carrying Patel, his daughter Maniben, and the Maharaja of Patiala from Delhi to Jaipur. The pilot had been ordered to fly at a low altitude due to turbulence. During the flight, loss of power in an engine caused the pilot to make an emergency landing in a desert area in Rajasthan. Owing to the aircraft's flying at a low altitude, the pilot was unable to send a distress call with the aircraft's VHF radio, nor could he use his HF equipment as the crew lacked a trained signaller. With all passengers safe, Patel and others tracked down a nearby village and local officials. A subsequent RIAF court of inquiry headed by Group Captain (later Air Chief Marshal and Chief of the Air Staff) Pratap Chandra Lal concluded the forced landing had been caused by fuel starvation. When Patel returned to Delhi, thousands of Congressmen gave him a resounding welcome. In Parliament, MPs gave a long standing ovation to Patel, stopping proceedings for half an hour.*

## Death

*Patel's health declined rapidly through the summer of 1949. He later began coughing blood, whereupon Maniben began limiting his meetings and working hours and arranged for a personalised medical staff to begin attending to Patel. The then Chief Minister of West Bengal, Dr. Bidhan Chandra Roy heard Patel make jokes about his impending end, and in a private meeting Patel frankly admitted to his ministerial colleague N. V. Gadgil that he was not going to live much longer. Patel's health worsened after 2 November, when he began losing consciousness frequently and was confined to his bed. He was flown to Bombay on 12 December on advice from Dr Roy, to recuperate as his condition was deemed critical. Nehru, Rajagopalachari, Rajendra Prasad, and Menon all came to see him off at the airport in Delhi. Patel was extremely weak and had to be carried onto the aircraft in a chair. In Bombay, large crowds gathered at Santacruz Airport to greet him. To spare him from this stress, the aircraft landed at Juhu Aerodrome, where Chief Minister B. G. Kher and Morarji Desai were present to receive him with a car belonging to the Governor of Bombay that took Vallabhbhai to Birla House.*

*After suffering a massive heart attack (his second), Patel died on 15 December 1950 at Birla House in Bombay. In an unprecedented and unrepeated gesture, on the day after his death more than 1,500 officers of India's civil and police services congregated to mourn at Patel's residence in Delhi and pledged "complete loyalty and unremitting zeal" in India's service. Numerous governments and world leaders sent messages of condolence upon Patel's death, including Trygve Lie, the Secretary-General of the United Nations, President Sukarno of Indonesia, Prime Minister Liaquat Ali Khan of Pakistan and Prime Minister Clement Attlee of the United Kingdom.*

*In homage to Patel, Prime Minister Jawaharlal Nehru declared a week of national mourning. Patel's cremation was planned at Girgaum Chowpatty, but this was changed to Sonapur (now Marine Lines) when his daughter conveyed that it was his wish to be cremated like a common man in the same place as his wife and brother were earlier cremated. His cremation in Sonapur in Bombay was attended by a crowd of one million including Prime Minister Jawaharlal Nehru, Rajagopalachari and President Rajendra Prasad.*

# CHAPTER SIX

# MANGAL PANDEY

**Summary:**

*Mangal Pandey was an Indian soldier who played a key role in the events taking place just before the outbreak of the Indian rebellion of 1857. He was a sepoy (infantryman) in the 34th Bengal Native Infantry (BNI) regiment of the British East India Company. In 1984, the Indian government issued a postage stamp to remember him. His life and actions have also been portrayed in several cinematic productions.*

## MANGAL PANDEY

## Early life

*Mangal Pandey was born in Nagwa, a village of upper Ballia district, Ceded and Conquered Provinces (now in Uttar Pradesh), to a Hindu Brahmin family. Pandey had joined the Bengal Army in 1849. In March 1857, he was a private soldier (sepoy) in the 5th Company of the 34th Bengal Native Infantry.*

## Mutiny

*On the afternoon of 29 March 1857, Lieutenant Baugh, Adjutant of the 34th Bengal Native Infantry, then stationed at Barrackpore was informed that several men of his regiment were in an excited state. Further, it was reported to him that one of them, Mangal Pandey, was pacing in front of the regiment's guard room by the parade ground, armed with a loaded musket, calling upon the men to rebel and threatening to shoot the first European that he set eyes on. Testimony at a subsequent enquiry recorded that Pandey, unsettled by unrest amongst the sepoys and intoxicated by the narcotic bhang, had seized his weapons and ran to the quarter-guard building upon learning that a detachment of British soldiers was disembarking from a steamer near the cantonment.*

*Baugh immediately armed himself and galloped on his horse to the lines. Pandey took position behind the station gun, which was in front of the quarter-guard of the 34th, took aim at Baugh and fired. He missed Baugh, but the bullet struck his horse in the flank bringing both the horse and its rider down. Baugh quickly disentangled himself and, seizing one of his pistols, advanced towards Pandey and fired. He missed. Before Baugh could draw his sword, Pandey attacked him with a talwar (a heavy Indian sword) and closing with the adjutant, slashed Baugh on the shoulder and neck and brought him to the ground. It was then that another sepoy, Shaikh Paltu, intervened and tried to restrain Pandey even as he tried to reload his musket.*

*A British Sergeant-Major named Hewson had arrived on the parade ground before Baugh, summoned by an Indian naik (corporal). Hewson had ordered Jemadar Ishwari Prasad, the Indian officer in command of the quarter-guard, to arrest Pandey. To this, the jemadar stated that his NCOs had gone for help and that he could not take Pandey by himself. In response Hewson ordered Ishwari Prasad to fall in the guard with loaded weapons. In the meantime, Baugh had arrived on the field shouting 'Where is he? Where is he?' Hewson in reply called out to Baugh, 'Ride to the right, sir, for your life. The sepoy will fire at you!' At that point Pandey fired. Hewson had charged towards Pandey as he was fighting with Lieutenant Baugh. While confronting Pandey, Hewson was knocked to the ground from behind by a blow from Pandey's musket. The sound of the firing had brought other sepoys from the barracks; they remained mute spectators. At this juncture, Shaikh Paltu, while trying to defend the two Englishmen called upon the other sepoys to assist him. Assailed by sepoys who threw stones and shoes at his back, Shaikh Paltu called on the guard to help him hold Pandey, but they threatened to shoot him if he did not let go of the mutineer.*

*Some of the sepoys of the quarter-guard then advanced and struck at the two prostrate officers. They then threatened Shaikh Paltu and ordered him to release Pandey, whom he had been vainly trying to hold back. However, Paltu continued to hold Pandey until Baugh and the sergeant-major was able to get up. Himself wounded by now, Paltu was obliged to loosen his grip. He backed away in one direction and Baugh and Hewson in another, while being struck with the butt ends of the guards' muskets.*

## Intervention of General Hearsey

*In the meantime, a report of the incident had been carried to the commanding officer of the garrison Major-General John Bennet Hearsey, who then galloped to the quarter-guard with his two officer sons. It was now late afternoon and off-duty sepoys from the 43rd BNI, another regiment forming part of the Barrackpore brigade, had joined the crowd on the parade ground. While all were unarmed, Hearsey saw the possibility of general mutiny and sent orders to British troops to assemble at the Governor-General's residence. Taking in the chaotic scene at the bell-of-arms (arsenal) of the 34th BNI, Hearsey then rode up to the guard, drew his pistol and ordered them to do their duty by seizing Mangal Pandey. The General threatened to shoot the first man who disobeyed. The men of the quarter-guard fell in and followed Hearsey towards Pandey. Pandey then put the muzzle of the musket to his chest and discharged it by pressing the trigger with his foot. He collapsed bleeding, with his regimental jacket on fire, but not mortally wounded. With British and Indian officers now in control of the situation Mangal Pandey, "shivering and convulsed", was taken to the regimental hospital for treatment under guard.[8]*

## Trial and execution

*Pandey recovered and was brought to trial less than a week later. He stated steadfastly that he had mutinied on his own accord and that no other person had played any part in encouraging him. He was sentenced to death by hanging, along with Jemadar Ishwari Prasad, after three Sikh members of the quarter-guard testified that the latter had ordered them not to arrest Pandey. Mangal Pandey's execution took place on 8 April 1857, before all of the Indian and British units stationed in Barrackpore. The Delhi Gazette of 18 April described the hanging in some detail, stating that Pandey had refused to make any disclosures and that the occasion "had a most disheartening effect upon the sepoy regiments upon the ground". Jemadar Ishwari Prasad was separately executed by hanging on 21 April. In contrast to the silent Mangal Pandey, the jemadar expressed regret for his actions and urged the sepoys present to obey their officers in future.*

# CHAPTER SEVEN

# BAL GANGADHAR TILAK

**Summary:**

*Bal Gangadhar Tilak, endeared as Lokmanya Tilak, was an Indian nationalist, teacher, and an independence activist. He was one third of the Lal Bal Pal triumvirate. The British colonial authorities called him "The father of the Indian unrest". He was also conferred with the title of "Lokmanya", which means "accepted by the people as their leader". Mahatma Gandhi called him "The Maker of Modern India". Tilak was one of the first and strongest advocates of Swaraj ('self-rule') and a strong radical in Indian consciousness. He is known for his quote in Marathi: "Swaraj is my birthright and I shall have it!". He formed a close alliance with many Indian National Congress leaders including Bipin Chandra Pal, Lala Lajpat Rai, Aurobindo Ghosh, V. O. Chidambaram Pillai and Muhammad Ali Jinnah.*

**BAL GANGADHAR TILAK**

## Background

*Keshav Gangadhar Tilak was born on 23 July 1856 in an Marathi Hindu Chitpavan Brahmin family in Ratnagiri, the headquarters of the Ratnagiri district of present-day Maharashtra (then Bombay Presidency). His ancestral village was Chikhali. His father, Gangadhar Tilak was a school teacher and a Sanskrit scholar who died when Tilak was sixteen.*

*In 1871, Tilak was married to Tapibai when he was sixteen, a few months before his father's death. After marriage, her name was changed to Satyabhamabai. He obtained his Bachelor of Arts in first class in Mathematics from Deccan College of Pune in 1877. He left his M.A. course of study midway to join the L.L.B course instead, and in 1879 he obtained his L.L.B degree from Government Law College. After graduating, Tilak started teaching mathematics at a private school in Pune. Later, due to ideological differences with the colleagues in the new school, he withdrew and became a journalist. Tilak actively participated in public affairs. He stated: "Religion and practical life are not different. The real spirit is to make the country your family instead of working only for your own. The step beyond is to serve humanity and the next step is to serve God." Inspired by Vishnushastri Chiplunkar, he co-founded the New English school for secondary education in 1880 with a few of his college friends, including Gopal Ganesh Agarkar, Mahadev Ballal Namjoshi and Vishnushastri Chiplunkar. Their goal was to improve the quality of education for India's youth. The success of the school led them to set up the Deccan Education Society in 1884 to create a new system of education that taught young Indians nationalist ideas through an emphasis on Indian culture. The Society established the Fergusson College in 1885 for post-secondary studies. Tilak taught mathematics at Fergusson College. In 1890, Tilak left the Deccan Education Society for more openly political work. He began a mass movement towards independence by an emphasis on a religious and cultural revival.*

## Political career

*Tilak had a long political career agitating for Indian autonomy from British colonial rule. Before Gandhi, he was the most widely known Indian political leader. Unlike his fellow Maharashtrian contemporary, Gokhale, Tilak was considered a radical Nationalist but a Social conservative. He was imprisoned on a number of occasions that included a long stint at Mandalay. At one stage in his political life he was called "the father of Indian unrest" by British author Sir Valentine Chirol.*

## Indian National Congress

*Tilak joined the Indian National Congress in 1890. He opposed its moderate attitude, especially towards the fight for self-government. He was one of the most-eminent radicals at the time. In fact, it was the Swadeshi movement of 1905–1907 that resulted in the split within the Indian National Congress into the Moderates and the Extremists. During late 1896, a bubonic plague spread from Bombay to Pune, and by January 1897, it reached epidemic proportions. The British Indian Army was brought in to deal with the emergency and strict measures were employed to curb the plague, including the allowance of forced entry into private houses, the examination of the house's occupants, evacuation to hospitals and quarantine camps, removing and destroying personal possessions, and preventing patients from entering or leaving the city. By the end of May, the epidemic was under control. The measures used to curb the pandemic caused widespread resentment among the Indian public. Tilak took up this issue by publishing inflammatory articles in his paper Kesari (Kesari was written in Marathi, and "Maratha" was written in English), quoting the Hindu scripture, the Bhagavad Gita, to say that no blame could be attached to anyone who killed an oppressor without any thought of reward. Following this, on 22 June 1897, Commissioner Rand and another British officer, Lt. Ayerst were shot and killed by the Chapekar brothers and their other associates. According to Barbara and Thomas R. Metcalf, Tilak "almost surely concealed the identities of the perpetrators". Tilak was charged with incitement to murder and sentenced to 18 months imprisonment. When he emerged from prison in present-day Mumbai, he was revered as a martyr and a national hero. He adopted a new slogan coined by his associate Kaka Baptista: "Swaraj (self-rule) is my birthright and I shall have it." Following the Partition of Bengal, which was a strategy set out by Lord Curzon to weaken the nationalist movement, Tilak encouraged the Swadeshi movement and the Boycott movement. The movement consisted of the boycott of foreign goods and also the social boycott of any Indian who used foreign goods. The Swadeshi movement consisted of the usage of natively produced goods. Once foreign goods were boycotted, there was a gap which had to be filled by the production of those goods in India itself. Tilak said that the Swadeshi and Boycott movements are two sides of the same coin. Tilak opposed the moderate views of Gopal Krishna Gokhale, and was supported by fellow Indian nationalists Bipin Chandra Pal in Bengal and Lala Lajpat Rai in Punjab. They were referred to as the*

*"Lal-Bal-Pal triumvirate". In 1907, the annual session of the Congress Party was held at Surat, Gujarat. Trouble broke out over the selection of the new president of the Congress between the moderate and the radical sections of the party. The party split into the radicals faction, led by Tilak, Pal and Lajpat Rai, and the moderate faction. Nationalists like Aurobindo Ghose, V. O. Chidambaram Pillai were Tilak supporters. When asked in Calcutta whether he envisioned a Maratha-type of government for independent India, Tilak answered that the Maratha-dominated governments of 17th and 18th centuries were outmoded in the 20th century, and he wanted a genuine federal system for Free India where everyone was an equal partner. He added that only such a form of government would be able to safeguard India's freedom. He was the first Congress leader to suggest that Hindi written in the Devanagari script be accepted as the sole national language of India.*

## Sedition Charges

*During his lifetime among other political cases, Tilak had been tried for sedition charges in three times by British India Government—in 1897, 1909, and 1916. In 1897, Tilak was sentenced to 18 months in prison for preaching disaffection against the Raj. In 1909, he was again charged with sedition and intensifying racial animosity between Indians and the British. The Bombay lawyer Muhammad Ali Jinnah appeared in Tilak's defence but he was sentenced to six years in prison in Burma in a controversial judgement. In 1916 when for the third time Tilak was charged for sedition over his lectures on self-rule, Jinnah again was his lawyer and this time led him to acquittal in the case.*

## Imprisonment in Mandalay

*On 30 April 1908, two Bengali youths, Prafulla Chaki and Khudiram Bose, threw a bomb on a carriage at Muzzafarpur, to kill the Chief Presidency Magistrate Douglas Kingsford of Calcutta fame, but erroneously killed two women traveling in it. Chaki committed suicide when caught, and Bose was hanged. Tilak, in his paper Kesari, defended the revolutionaries and called for immediate Swaraj or self-rule. The Government swiftly charged him with sedition. At the conclusion of the trial, a special jury convicted him by 7:2 majority. The judge, Dinshaw D. Davar gave him a six years jail sentence to be served in Mandalay, Burma and a fine of ₹1,000 (US$12). On being asked by the judge whether he had anything to say, Tilak said: All that I wish to say is that, in spite of the verdict of the jury, I still maintain that I am innocent. There are higher powers that rule the destinies of men and nations; and I think, it may be the will of Providence that the cause I represent may be benefited more by my suffering than by my pen and tongue. Muhammad Ali Jinnah was his lawyer in the case. Justice Davar's judgement came under stern criticism in press and was seen against impartiality of British justice system. Justice Davar himself previously had appeared for Tilak in his first sedition case in 1897. In passing sentence, the judge indulged in some scathing strictures against Tilak's conduct.*

*He threw off the judicial restraint which, to some extent, was observable in his charge to the jury. He condemned the articles as "seething with sedition", as preaching violence, speaking of murders with approval. "You hail the advent of the bomb in India as if something had come to India for its good. I say, such journalism is a curse to the country". Tilak was sent to Mandalay from 1908 to 1914. While imprisoned, he continued to read and write, further developing his ideas on the Indian nationalist movement. While in the prison he wrote the Gita Rahasya. Many copies of which were sold, and the money was donated for the Indian Independence movement.*

## Life after Mandalay

*Tilak developed diabetes during his sentence in Mandalay prison. This and the general ordeal of prison life had mellowed him at his release on 16 June 1914. When World War I started in August of that year, Tilak cabled the King-Emperor George V of his support and turned his oratory to find new recruits for war efforts. He welcomed The Indian Councils Act, popularly known as Minto-Morley Reforms, which had been passed by British Parliament in May 1909, terming it as "a marked increase of confidence between the Rulers and the Ruled". It was his conviction that acts of violence actually diminished, rather than hastening, the pace of political reforms. He was eager for reconciliation with Congress and had abandoned his demand for direct action and settled for agitations "strictly by constitutional means" – a line that had long been advocated by his rival Gokhale. Tilak reunited with his fellow nationalists and rejoined the Indian National Congress during the Lucknow pact 1916. Tilak tried to convince Mohandas Gandhi to leave the idea of Total non-violence ("Total Ahimsa") and try to get self-rule ("Swarajya") by all means. Though Gandhi did not entirely concur with Tilak on the means to achieve self-rule and was steadfast in his advocacy of satyagraha, he appreciated Tilak's services to the country and his courage of conviction. After Tilak lost a civil suit against Valentine Chirol and incurred pecuniary loss, Gandhi even called upon Indians to contribute to the Tilak Purse Fund started with the objective of defraying the expenses incurred by Tilak.*

## All India Home Rule League

*Tilak helped found the All India Home Rule League in 1916–18, with G. S. Khaparde and Annie Besant. After years of trying to reunite the moderate and radical factions, he gave up and focused on the Home Rule League, which sought self-rule. Tilak travelled from village to village for support from farmers and locals to join the movement towards self-rule. Tilak was impressed by the Russian Revolution, and expressed his admiration for Vladimir Lenin. The league had 1400 members in April 1916, and by 1917 membership had grown to approximately 32,000. Tilak started his Home Rule League in Maharashtra, Central Provinces, and Karnataka and Berar region.*

*Besant's League was active in the rest of India.*

## Thoughts and views

### *Religio-Political Views*

*Tilak sought to unite the Indian population for mass political action throughout his life. For this to happen, he believed there needed to be a comprehensive justification for anti-British pro-Hindu activism. For this end, he sought justification in the supposed original principles of the Ramayana and the Bhagavad Gita. He named this call to activism karma-yoga or the yoga of action. In his interpretation, the Bhagavad Gita reveals this principle in the conversation between Krishna and Arjuna when Krishna exhorts Arjuna to fight his enemies (which in this case included many members of his family) because it is his duty. In Tilak's opinion, the Bhagavad Gita provided a strong justification of activism. However, this conflicted with the mainstream exegesis of the text at the time which was dominated by renunciate views and the idea of acts purely for God. This was represented by the two mainstream views at the time by Ramanuja and Adi Shankara. To find support for this philosophy, Tilak wrote his own interpretations of the relevant passages of the Gita and backed his views using Jnanadeva's commentary on the Gita, Ramanuja's critical commentary and his own translation of the Gita.*

## Social views against women

*Tilak was strongly opposed to liberal trends emerging in Pune such as women's rights and social reforms against untouchability. Tilak vehemently opposed the establishment of the first Native girls High school (now called Huzurpaga) in Pune in 1885 and its curriculum using his newspapers, the Mahratta and Kesari. Tilak was also opposed to intercaste marriage, particularly the match where an upper caste woman married a lower caste man. In the case of Deshasthas, Chitpawans and Karhades, he encouraged these three Maharashtrian Brahmin groups to give up "caste exclusiveness" and intermarry.[a] Tilak officially opposed the age of consent bill which raised the age of marriage from ten to twelve for girls, however he was willing to sign a circular that increased age of marriage for girls to sixteen and twenty for boys. Child bride Rukhmabai was married at the age of eleven but refused to go and live with her husband. The husband sued for restitution of conjugal rights, initially lost but appealed the decision. On 4 March 1887, Justice Farran, using interpretations of Hindu laws, ordered Rukhmabai to "go live with her husband or face six months of imprisonment". Tilak approved of this decision of the court and said that the court was following Hindu Dharmaśāstras. Rukhmabai responded that she would rather face imprisonment than obey the verdict. Her marriage was later dissolved by Queen Victoria. Later, she went on to receive her Doctor of Medicine degree from the London School of Medicine for Women. In 1890, when an eleven-year-old Phulamani Bai died while having sexual intercourse with her much older husband, the Parsi social reformer Behramji Malabari supported the Age of Consent Act, 1891 to raise the age of a girl's eligibility for marriage. Tilak opposed the Bill and said that the Parsis as well as the English had no jurisdiction over the (Hindu) religious matters. He blamed the girl for having "defective female organs" and questioned how the husband could be "persecuted diabolically for doing a harmless act". He called the girl one of those "dangerous freaks of nature". Tilak did not have a progressive view when it came to gender relations. He did not believe that Hindu women should get a modern education. Rather, he had a more conservative view, believing that women were meant to be homemakers who had to subordinate themselves to the needs of their husbands and children. Tilak refused to sign a petition for the abolition of untouchability in 1918, two years before his death, although he had spoken against it earlier in a meeting.*

## Esteem for Swami Vivekananda

*Tilak and Swami Vivekananda had great mutual respect and esteem for each other. They met accidentally while travelling by train in 1892 and Tilak had Vivekananda as a guest in his house. A person who was present there(Basukaka), heard that it was agreed between Vivekananda and Tilak that Tilak would work towards nationalism in the "political" arena, while Vivekananda would work for nationalism in the "religious" arena. When Vivekananda died at a young age, Tilak expressed great sorrow and paid tributes to him in the Kesari.*

*Tilak said about Vivekananda:*

*"No Hindu, who, has the interests of Hinduism at his heart, could help feeling grieved over Vivekananda's samadhi. Vivekananda, in short, had taken the work of keeping the banner of Advaita philosophy forever flying among all the nations of the world and made them realize the true greatness of Hindu religion and of the Hindu people. He had hoped that he would crown his achievement with the fulfillment of this task by virtue of his learning, eloquence, enthusiasm and sincerity, just as he had laid a secure foundation for it; but with Swami's samadhi, these hopes have gone. Thousands of years ago, another saint, Shankaracharya, who, showed to the world the glory and greatness of Hinduism. At the fag of the 19<sup>th</sup> century, the second Shankaracharya is Vivekananda, who, showed to the world the glory of Hinduism. His work has yet to be completed. We have lost our glory, our independence, everything."*

## Caste Issues

*Shahu, the ruler of the princely state of Kolhapur, had several conflicts with Tilak as the latter agreed with the Brahmins decision of Puranic rituals for the Marathas that were intended for Shudras. Tilak even suggested that the Marathas should be "content" with the Shudra status assigned to them by the Brahmins. Tilak's newspapers, as well as the press in Kolhapur, criticized Shahu for his caste prejudice and his unreasoned hostility towards Brahmins. These included serious allegations such as sexual assaults by Shahu against four Brahmin women. An English woman named Lady Minto was petitioned to help them. The agent of Shahu had blamed these allegations on the "troublesome brahmins". Tilak and another Brahmin suffered from the confiscation of estates by Shahu, the first during a quarrel between Shahu and the Shankaracharya of Sankareshwar and later in another issue.*

*Bal Gangadhar Tilak was released from prison on 16 June 1914. He commented:*

**'If we can prove to the non-Brahmins, by example, that we are wholly on their side in their demands from the Government, I am sure that in times to come their agitation, now based on social inequality, will merge into our struggle.'**

**'If a God were to tolerate untouchability, I would not recognize him as God at all.'**

## Social contributions

*Tilak started two weeklies, Kesari ("The Lion") in Marathi and Mahratta in English (sometimes referred as 'Maratha' in Academic Study Books) in 1880–1881 with Gopal Ganesh Agarkar as the first editor. By this he was recognized as 'awakener of*

*India', as Kesari later became a daily and continues publication to this day. In 1894, Tilak transformed the household worshipping of Ganesha into a grand public event (Sarvajanik Ganeshotsav). The celebrations consisted of several days of processions, music, and food. They were organized by the means of subscriptions by neighbourhood, caste, or occupation. Students often would celebrate Hindu and national glory and address political issues; including patronage of Swadeshi goods. In 1895, Tilak founded the Shri Shivaji Fund Committee for the celebration of "Shiv Jayanti", the birth anniversary of Shivaji, the founder of the Maratha Empire. The project also had the objective of funding the reconstruction of the tomb (Samadhi) of Shivaji at Raigad Fort. For this second objective, Tilak established the Shri Shivaji Raigad Smarak Mandal along with Senapati Khanderao Dabhade II of Talegaon Dabhade, who became the founder President of the Mandal.*

*The events like the Ganapati festival and Shiv Jayanti were used by Tilak to build a national spirit beyond the circle of the educated elite in opposition to colonial rule. But it also exacerbated Hindu-Muslim differences. The festival organizers would urge Hindus to protect cows and boycott the Muharram celebrations organized by Shi'a Muslims, in which Hindus had formerly often participated. Thus, although the celebrations were meant to be a way to oppose colonial rule, they also contributed to religious tensions. Contemporary Marathi Hindu nationalist parties like the Shiv Sena took up his reverence for Shivaji. However, Indian Historian, Uma Chakravarti cites Professor Gordon Johnson and states "It is significant that even at the time when Tilak was making political use of Shivaji the question of conceding Kshatriya status to him as Maratha was resisted by the conservative Brahmins including Tilak. While Shivaji was a Brave man, all his bravery, it was argued, did not give him the right to a status that very nearly approached that of a Brahmin. Further, the fact that Shivaji worshiped the Brahmanas in no way altered social relations, 'since it was as a Shudra he did it – as a Shudra the servant, if not the slave, of the Brahmin'".*

*The Deccan Education Society that Tilak founded with others in the 1880s still runs Institutions in Pune like the Fergusson College.[65] The Swadeshi movement started by Tilak at the beginning of the 20th century became part of the Independence movement until that goal was achieved in 1947. One can even say Swadeshi remained part of Indian Government policy until the 1990s when the Congress Government liberalised the economy. Tilak said, "I regard India as my Motherland and my Goddess, the people in India are my kith and kin, and loyal and steadfast work for their political and social emancipation is my highest religion and duty"*

# VINAYAK SAVARKAR

**Summary:**

*Vinayak Damodar Savarkar was an Indian politician, activist and writer. Savarkar developed the Hindu nationalist political ideology of Hindutva while confined at Ratnagiri in 1922. He was a leading figure in the Hindu Mahasabha. The prefix "Veer" has been applied to his name by his followers. Savarkar began his political activities as a high school student and continued to do so at Fergusson College in Pune. He and his brother founded a secret society called Abhinav Bharat Society. When he went to the United Kingdom for his law studies, he involved himself with organizations such as India House and the Free India Society. He also published books advocating complete Indian independence by revolutionary means. One of the books he published called The Indian War of Independence about the Indian Rebellion of 1857 was banned by the British colonial authorities.*

**VEER SAVARKAR**

## Background

*Vinayak Damodar Savarkar was born on 28 May 1883 in the Marathi Hindu Chitpavan Brahmin family, to Damodar and Radhabai Savarkar in the village of Bhagur, near the city of Nashik, Maharashtra. He had three other siblings namely Ganesh, Narayan, and a sister named Maina. Savarkar began his activism as a high school student. When he was 12, he led fellow students in an attack on his village mosque following Hindu-Muslim riots, stating: "We vandalized the mosque to our heart's content." In 1903, in Nashik, Savarkar and his older brother Ganesh Savarkar founded the Mitra Mela, an underground revolutionary organization, which became Abhinav Bharat Society in 1906. Abhinav Bharat's main objectives were to overthrow British rule and reviving Hindu pride.*

## Student activist

*Savarkar continued his political activism as a student at Fergusson College in Pune. Savarkar was greatly influenced by the radical Nationalist leader, Lokmanya Tilak. Tilak was in turn impressed with the young student and helped him obtain the Shivaji Scholarship in 1906 for his law studies in London. To protest against Bengal partition of 1905, Savarkar led foreign-clothes bonfire in India with other students in presence of Bal Gangadhar Tilak.*

## London years

*In London, Savarkar got involved with organizations such as India House and the Free India Society. He also published books advocating complete Indian independence by revolutionary means. One of the books he published called The Indian War of Independence about the Indian Rebellion of 1857 was banned by the British colonial authorities. Savarkar was influenced by the life and thinking of Italian Nationalist leader, Giuseppe Mazzini. During his stay in London, Savarkar translated Mazzini's biography in Marathi. He also influenced thinking of a fellow student called Madanlal Dhingra. In 1909, Dhingra assassinated Curzon Wyllie, a colonial officer. It is alleged by Mark Juergensmeyer that Savarkar supplied the gun which Dhingra used. Juergensmeyer further alleged that Savarkar supplied the words for Dhingra's last statement before he went to the gallows for the murder. Savarkar met Mohandas Gandhi for the first time in London shortly after Curzon-Wyllie's assassination. During his stay, Gandhi debated Savarkar and other nationalists in London on the futility of fighting the colonial state through acts of terrorism and guerilla warfare.*

## Arrest and transportation to India

*In India, Ganesh Savarkar organized an armed revolt against the Morley-Minto reforms of 1909, and was sentenced to life imprisonment on the Andaman islands. Around the same time Vinayak Savarkar was accused of participating in a conspiracy to overthrow the British government in India by organizing murders of various officials. Hoping to evade arrest, Savarkar moved to Bhikaiji Cama's home in Paris, but against advice from his friends, returned to London. On 13 March 1910, he was arrested in London on multiple charges, including procurement and distribution of arms, waging war against the state, and delivering seditious speeches. At the time of his arrest, he was carrying several revolutionary texts, including copies of his own banned books. In addition, the British government had evidence that he had smuggled 20 Browning handguns into India, one of which Anant Laxman Kanhere used to assassinate the Nasik district's collector A.M.T. Jackson in December 1909. During the trial of Nasik Conspiracy Case 1910, government's advocate alleged that Savarkar was a moving part and inspiration behind assassination of Jackson. A Bombay court tried him in the Nasik conspiracy case and sentenced him for life-imprisonment and transported him to the notorious Cellular Jail of Andaman Island and forfeited his property. Although his alleged crimes were committed both in Britain, as well as India, the British authorities decided to try him in India. He was accordingly put on the commercial ship Morea with a police escort for his transport to India. When the ship docked in the French Mediterranean port of Marseille, Savarkar escaped by jumping from the ship's window, swam to the French shore, and asked for political asylum. The French port officials ignored his pleas, and handed him back to his British captors. When the French government came to know of this incidence, they asked for Savarkar to be brought back to France, and lodged an appeal with the Permanent Court of Arbitration. Savarkar's arrest at Marseilles caused the French government to protest against the British, arguing that the British could not recover Savarkar unless they took appropriate legal proceedings for his rendition. The dispute came before the Permanent Court of International Arbitration in 1910, and it gave its decision in 1911. The case excited much controversy as was reported widely by the French press, and it considered it involved an interesting international question of the right of asylum. The*

*Court held, firstly, that since there was a pattern of collaboration between the two countries regarding the possibility of Savarkar's escape in Marseilles and there was neither force nor fraud in inducing the French authorities to return Savarkar to them, the British authorities did not have to hand him back to the French for the latter to hold rendition proceedings. On the other hand, the tribunal also observed that there had been an "irregularity" in Savarkar's arrest and delivery over to the Indian Army Military Police guard.*

## Trial and sentence

*Arriving in Bombay, Savarkar was taken to the Yervada Central Jail in Pune. The trial before the special tribunal was started on 10 September 1910. One of the charges on Savarkar was the abetment to murder of Nashik Collector A. M. T. Jackson. The second was waging a conspiracy under Indian penal code 121-A against the King Emperor. Following the two trials, Savarkar, then aged 28, was convicted and sentenced to 50-years imprisonment and transported on 4 July 1911 to the infamous Cellular Jail in the Andaman and Nicobar Islands. He was considered by the British government as a political prisoner.*

## Clemency Petitions

*1911*

*Savarkar applied to the Bombay Government for certain concessions in connection with his sentences. However, by Government letter No. 2022, dated 4 April 1911, his application was rejected and he was informed that the question of remitting the second sentence of transportation for life would be considered in due course on the expiry of the first sentence of transportation for life. A month after arriving in the Cellular Jail, Andaman and Nicobar Islands, Savarkar submitted his first clemency petition on 30 August 1911. This petition was rejected on 3 September 1911.*

## 1913

*Savarkar submitted his next clemency petition on 14 November 1913 and presented it personally to the Home Member of the Governor General's council, Sir Reginald Craddock. In his letter, he described himself as a "prodigal son" longing to return to the "parental doors of the government". He wrote that his release from the jail will recast the faith of many Indians in the British rule. Also, he said "Moreover, my conversion to the constitutional line would bring back all those misled young men in India and abroad who were once looking up to me as their guide. I am ready to serve the government in any capacity they like, for as my conversion is conscientious so I hope my future conduct would be. By keeping me in jail, nothing can be got in comparison to what would be otherwise."*

## *1917*

*In 1917, Savarkar submitted another clemency petition, this time for a general amnesty of all political prisoners. Savarkar was informed on 1 February 1918 that the clemency petition was placed before the British colonial government. In December 1919, there was a Royal proclamation by King George V. The Paragraph 6 of this proclamation included a declaration of Royal clemency to political offenders. In view of Royal proclamation, Savarkar submitted his fourth clemency petition to the British colonial government on 30 March 1920, in which he stated that "So far from believing in the militant school of the Bukanin type, I do not contribute even to the peaceful and philosophical anarchism of a Kuropatkin or a Tolstoy. And as to my revolutionary tendencies in the past- it is not only now for the object of sharing the clemency but years before this have I informed of and written to the Government in my petitions (1918, 1914) about my firm intention to abide by the constitution and stand by it as soon as a beginning was made to frame it by Mr. Montagu. Since that the Reforms and then the Proclamation have only confirmed me in my views and recently I have publicly avowed my faith in and readiness to stand by the side of orderly and constitutional development." This petition was rejected on 12 July 1920 by the British colonial government. After considering the petition, the British colonial government contemplated releasing Ganesh Savarkar but not Vinayak Savarkar. The rationale for doing so was stated as follows:*

*It may be observed that if Ganesh is released and Vinayak is retained in custody, the latter will become in some measure a hostage for the former, who will see that his own misconduct does not jeopardize his brother's chances of release at some future date. Savarkar signed a statement endorsing his trial, verdict, and British law, and renouncing violence, a bargain for freedom.*

## Ratnagiri years under restricted freedom

*On 2 May 1921, the Savarkar brothers were transferred from Andaman to mainland India with Vinayak being sent to a jail in Ratnagiri, and Ganesh to Bijapur Jail. During his incarceration in Ratnagiri jail in 1922, Vinayak wrote his "Essentials of Hindutva" that formulated his theory of Hindutva. Ganesh (Babarao) Savarkar was unconditionally released from jail in 1922. On 6 January 1924 Vinayak was released, but was restricted to Ratnagiri District. Soon after his release, he started working on the consolidation of Hindu society or Hindu Sangathan. The colonial authorities provided a bungalow for him and he was allowed visitors. During his internment, he met influential people such as Mahatma Gandhi and B. R. Ambedkar. Nathuram Godse, who later assassinated Gandhi, also met Savarkar for the first time as a nineteen-year-old in 1929. Savarkar became a prolific writer during his years of restricted freedom in Ratnagiri. His publishers, however, needed to have a disclaimer that they were wholly divorced from politics. Savarkar remained restricted to Ratnagiri district until 1937.*

*At that time, he was unconditionally released by the newly elected government of Bombay presidency.*

## Leader of the Hindu Mahasabha

*Savarkar as president of the Hindu Mahasabha, during the Second World War, advanced the slogan "Hinduize all Politics and Militarize Hindudom" and decided to support the British war effort in India seeking military training for the Hindus. When the Congress launched the Quit India movement in 1942, Savarkar criticised it and asked Hindus to stay active in the war effort and not disobey the government; he also urged the Hindus to enlist in the armed forces to learn the "arts of war". Hindu Mahasabha under Savarkar's leadership organized Hindu Militarization Boards which recruited armed forces for helping the British in World War 2. He assailed the British proposals for transfer of power, attacking both the Congress and the British for making concessions to Muslim separatists. Soon after independence, Syama Prasad Mukherjee resigned as vice-president of the Hindu Mahasabha dissociating himself from its Akhand Hindustan (Undivided India) plank, which implied undoing partition.*

## Opposition to Quit India Movement

*Under Savarkar, the Hindu Mahasabha openly opposed the call for the Quit India Movement and boycotted it officially. Savarkar even went to the extent of writing a letter titled "Stick to your Posts", in which he instructed Hindu Sabhaites who happened to be "members of municipalities, local bodies, legislatures or those serving in the army ... to stick to their posts" across the country, and not to join the Quit India Movement at any cost.*

## Alliance with Muslim League and others

*The Indian National Congress won a massive victory in the 1937 Indian provincial elections, decimating the Muslim League and the Hindu Mahasabha. However, in 1939, the Congress ministries resigned in protest against Viceroy Lord Linlithgow's action of declaring India to be a belligerent in the Second World War without consulting the Indian people. This led to the Hindu Mahasabha, under Savarkar's presidency, joining hands with the Muslim League and other parties to form governments, in certain provinces. Such coalition governments were formed in Sindh, NWFP, and Bengal. In Sindh, Hindu Mahasabha members joined Ghulam Hussain Hidayatullah's Muslim League government. In Savarkar's own words, witness the fact that only recently in Sind, the Sind-Hindu-Sabha on invitation had taken the responsibility of joining hands with the League itself in running coalition government. In the North West Frontier Province, Hindu Mahasabha members joined hands with Sardar Aurangzeb Khan of the Muslim League to form a government in 1943. The Mahasabha member of the cabinet was Finance Minister Mehar Chand Khanna. In Bengal, Hindu Mahasabha joined the Krishak Praja Party led*

*Progressive Coalition ministry of Fazlul Haq in December 1941. Savarkar appreciated the successful functioning of the coalition government.*

## Arrest and acquittal in Gandhi's assassination

*Following the assassination of Gandhi on 30 January 1948, police arrested the assassin Nathuram Godse and his alleged accomplices and conspirators. He was a member of the Hindu Mahasabha and of the Rashtriya Swayamsevak Sangh. Godse was the editor of Agrani – Hindu Rashtra, a Marathi daily from Pune which was run by the company "The Hindu Rashtra Prakashan Ltd" (The Hindu Nation Publications). This company had contributions from such eminent persons as Gulabchand Hirachand, Bhalji Pendharkar, and Jugalkishore Birla. Savarkar had invested ₹ 15000 in the company. Savarkar, a former president of the Hindu Mahasabha, was arrested on 5 February 1948, from his house in Shivaji Park, and kept under detention in the Arthur Road Prison, Bombay. He was charged with murder, conspiracy to murder, and abetment to murder. A day before his arrest, Savarkar in a public written statement, as reported in The Times of India, Bombay dated 7 February 1948, termed Gandhi's assassination a fratricidal crime, endangering India's existence as a nascent nation. The mass of papers seized from his house had revealed nothing that could remotely be connected with Gandhi's murder.: Chapter 12 Due to lack of evidence, Savarkar was arrested under the Preventive Detention Act. :Chapter 11*

## Badge's testimony

*Godse claimed full responsibility for planning and carrying out the assassination. However, according to the Approver Digambar Badge, on 17 January 1948, Nathuram Godse went to have a last darshan (audience/interview) with Savarkar in Bombay before the assassination. While Badge and Shankar waited outside, Nathuram and Apte went in. On coming out Apte told Badge that Savarkar blessed them "Yashasvi houn ya" ("यशस्वी होऊन या", be successful and return). Apte also said that Savarkar predicted that Gandhi's 100 years were over and there was no doubt that the task would be successfully finished. However Badge's testimony was not accepted as the approver's evidence lacked independent corroboration and hence Savarkar was acquitted.*

*In the last week of August 1974, Mr. Manohar Malgonkar saw Digamber Badge several times and in particular, questioned him about the veracity of his testimony against Savarkar.:Notes Badge insisted to Mr. Manohar Malgonkar that "even though he had blurted out the full story of the plot as far as he knew, without much persuasion, he had put up a valiant struggle against being made to testify against Savarkar". :Chapter 12 In the end, Badge gave in. He agreed to say on oath that he saw Nathuram Godse and Apte with Savarkar and that Savarkar, within*

*Badge's hearing, had blessed their venture. : Chapter 12*

## Kapur commission

*On 12 November 1964, at a religious program organized in Pune to celebrate the release of Gopal Godse, Madanlal Pahwa and Vishnu Karkare from jail after the expiry of their sentences, G. V. Ketkar, grandson of Bal Gangadhar Tilak, former editor of Kesari and then editor of "Tarun Bharat", who presided over the function, gave information of a conspiracy to kill Gandhi, about which he professed knowledge six months before the act. Ketkar was arrested. A public furor ensued both outside and inside the Maharashtra Legislative Assembly and both houses of the Indian parliament. Under the pressure of 29 members of parliament and public opinion the then Union home minister Gulzarilal Nanda appointed Gopal Swarup Pathak, M. P. and a senior advocate of the Supreme Court of India as a Commission of Inquiry to re-investigate the conspiracy to murder Gandhi. The central government intended on conducting a thorough inquiry with the help of old records in consultation with the government of Maharashtra. Pathak was given three months to conduct his inquiry; subsequently, Jevanlal Kapur, a retired judge of the Supreme Court of India, was appointed chairman of the commission. The commission's reinvestigation saw Savarkar's secretary and bodyguard to have testified that Savarkar met with Godse and Apte right before Gandhi was killed. The commission was*

*provided with evidence not produced in the court;
especially the testimony of two of Savarkar's close
aides – Appa Ramachandra Kasar, his bodyguard, and
Gajanan Vishnu Damle, his secretary. The testimony
of Mr. Kasar and Mr. Damle was already recorded
by Bombay police on 4 March 1948, but apparently,
these testimonies were not presented before the court
during the trial. In these testimonies, it is said that
Godse and Apte visited Savarkar on or about 23 or
24 January, which was when they returned from Delhi
after the bomb incident. Damle deposed that Godse
and Apte saw Savarkar in the middle of January and
sat with him (Savarkar) in his garden. The C. I. D.
Bombay was keeping vigil on Savarkar from 21 to
30 January 1948. The crime report from C. I. D.
does not mention Godse or Apte meeting Savarkar
during this time. The arrest of Savarkar was mainly
based on approver Digambar Badge's testimony. The
commission did not re-interview Digambar Badge. At
the time of inquiry of the commission, Badge was alive
and working in Bombay.*

## Later years

*After Gandhi's assassination, Savarkar's home in
Dadar, Bombay was stoned by angry mobs. After he
was acquitted of the allegations related to Gandhi's
assassination and released from jail, Savarkar was
arrested by the government for making "Hindu
nationalist speeches"; he was released after agreeing
to give up political activities. He continued addressing
the social and cultural elements of Hindutva. He
resumed political activism after the ban on it was*

*lifted; it was however limited until his death in 1966 because of ill health. In 1956, he opposed B.R. Ambedkar's conversion to Buddhism calling it a "useless act", to which Ambedkar responded by publicly questioning the use of epithet 'Veer' (meaning brave) by Savarkar. On 22 November 1957, Raja Mahendra Pratap moved a bill in Lok Sabha to recognise the service to the country of people like Vir Savarkar, Barindra Kumar Ghosh and Bhupendranath Datta. But the bill was defeated with 48 votes favouring it and 75 against it. This bill was also supported by communist leader like A. K. Gopalan.*

## Death

*On 8 November 1963, Savarkar's wife, Yamunabai, died. On 1 February 1966, Savarkar renounced medicines, food, and water which was termed as prayopavesha (fast until death). Before his death, he had written an article titled "Atmahatya Nahi Atmaarpan" in which he argued that when one's life mission is over and the ability to serve society is left no more, it is better to end the life at will rather than waiting for death. His condition was described to have become as "extremely serious" before his death on 26 February 1966 at his residence in Bombay (now Mumbai), and that he faced difficulty in breathing; efforts to revive him failed, and was declared dead at 11:10 a.m. (IST) that day. Prior to his death, Savarkar had asked his relatives to perform only his funeral and do away with the rituals of the 10th and*

13$^{th}$ *day of the Hindu faith. Accordingly, his last rites were performed at an electric crematorium in Bombay's Sonapur locality by his son Vishwas the following day. There was no official mourning by the Maharashtra Pradesh Congress Committee or the central government in Delhi during the time of his death. Not a single minister from the Maharashtra Cabinet showed up to pay homage and respect to Savarkar. The political indifference to Savarkar has also continued after his death. After the death of Nehru, Prime Minister Shastri, started to pay him a monthly pension.*

# CHAPTER NINE

# NATHURAM GODSE

**Summary:**

*Nathuram Vinayak Godse was a Hindu nationalist who on 30 January 1948 assassinated Mahatma Gandhi. Godse was a member of the political party, the Hindu Mahasabha; and a member of the Rashtriya Swayamsevak Sangh (RSS), a right-wing Hindu paramilitary volunteer organisation; and a populariser of the work of his mentor Vinayak Damodar Savarkar, who had created the ideology of Hindutva. Godse together with Narayan Apte made two unsuccessful attempts to assassinate Mahatma Gandhi in 1944 before they succeeded the third time in 1948. After the 1948 assassination, Godse claimed Gandhi favoured the political demands of British India's Muslims during the partition of India of 1947.*

**NATHURAM GODSE**

## Background

*Nathuram Vinayakrao Godse was born into a Maharashtrian Chitpavan Brahmin family. His father, Vinayak Vamanrao Godse, was a postal employee; his mother was Lakshmi. At birth, he was named Ramachandra. Nathuram was given his name due to his parents' fear that a curse targeted their male children, caused by the loss of their three previous sons. Young Ramachandra was therefore brought up as a girl for the first few years of his life, including having his nose pierced and being made to wear a nose-ring (nath in Marathi). It was then that he earned the nickname "Nathuram" (literally "Ram with a nose-ring"). After his younger brother was born, they switched to treating him as a boy. Godse attended the local school at Baramati through the fifth standard, after which he was sent to live with an aunt in Pune so that he could study at an English-language school.*

## Political career and beliefs

*Godse dropped out of high school and became an activist with Hindu nationalist organisations Rashtriya Swayamsevak Sangh (RSS; National Volunteer Organisation) and Hindu Mahasabha, although the exact dates of his membership are uncertain.*

## RSS membership

*Godse joined RSS in Sangli (Maharashtra) in 1932 as a boudhik karyawah (ground worker), and simultaneously remained a member of the Hindu Mahasabha, both right-wing organisations. He often wrote articles in newspapers to publicise his thoughts. During this time, Godse and M. S. Golwalkar, later RSS chief, often worked together, and they translated Babarao Savarkar's book "Rashtra Mimansa" into English. They had a falling out when Golwalkar took the entire credit for this translation. In the early 1940s, Godse formed his own organisation, "Hindu Rashtra Dal" on the Vijayadashami day of 1942, though he continued to remain a member of the RSS and Hindu Mahasabha. In 1946, Godse claimed to have left the RSS and moved to the Hindu Mahasabha over the issue of the partition of India. However, historical sources do not corroborate this claim; an investigation published by The Caravan in January 2020 revealed that up until his final days, Godse was listed as a member in records kept by the RSS of meetings that took place long after he was supposed to have left the organisation. His family has also said that he had never left the RSS, highlighting that he held membership at the RSS as well as the Hindu Mahasabha. Godse's 1946 claim is also refuted by his first deposition in Marathi after he assassinated Gandhi, where he says that while he did join the Hindu Mahasabha, "I remained active in Rashtriya Swayamsevak Sangh."*

## Assassination of Mahatma Gandhi

*In May 1944, Godse attempted to assassinate Gandhi with a knife. He led a group of 15 to 20 young men who rushed at Gandhi during a prayer meeting at Panchgani. Godse and his group were prevented by the crowds from reaching Gandhi. He was released due to Gandhi's own policy of declining to press criminal charges. On September 1944, Godse again led another group to block Gandhi's passage from Sevagram to Mumbai. This time Godse was arrested with a dagger and he uttered threats to kill Gandhi. He was released again owing to Gandhi's policy of not pressing criminal charges. At 05:05 PM on 30 January 1948, as Gandhi made his way to a prayer meeting on a raised lawn behind Birla House, a mansion in New Delhi, where he was staying, Godse stepped out of the crowd flanking his path to the dais. He fired three bullets into Gandhi's chest. Gandhi fell immediately, sending the attendant crowd into a state of shock. Herbert Reiner Jr., a 32-year-old vice-consul at the new American embassy in Delhi, was the first to rush forward and grasp Godse by the shoulders, spinning him into the arms of some military personnel, who disarmed him. Reiner then held Godse by the neck and shoulders until he was taken away by the military and police. Reiner reported later that in the moments before he apprehended him, Godse looked a little stunned at how easily he had carried out his plan. Gandhi was taken back to his room in Birla House, where he died soon thereafter.*

## Trial and execution

*Godse was put on trial at the Punjab High Court, at Peterhoff, Shimla. On 8 November 1949, he was sentenced to death. Although pleas for commutation were made by Gandhi's two sons, Manilal Gandhi and Ramdas Gandhi, they were turned down by India's prime minister Jawaharlal Nehru, deputy prime minister Vallabhbhai Patel and Governor-General Chakravarti Rajagopalachari, and Godse was hanged at Ambala Central Jail on 15 November 1949.*

# RANI LAKSHMI BAI

**Summary:**

*Lakshmibai Newalkar, the Rani of Jhansi was the Maharani consort of the princely state of Jhansi in the Maratha Empire from 1843 to 1853 by marriage to Maharaja Gangadhar Rao Newalkar. She was one of the leading figures in the Indian Rebellion of 1857, who became a national hero and symbol of resistance to the British rule in India for Indian nationalists.*

**RANI LAKSHMI BAI**

## Background

*Rani Lakshmi Bai was born in the town of Banares (now Varanasi) into a Marathi Karhade Brahmin family. She was named Manikarnika Tambe and was nicknamed Manu. Her father was Moropant Tambe and her mother Bhagirathi Sapre (Bhagirathi Bai). Her parents came from the Tambe village of the Guhagar taluka located in the Ratnagiri district of modern-day Maharashtra. Her mother died when she was five years old. Her father was a Commander during the war of Kalyanpranth. Her father worked for Peshwa Baji Rao II of Bithoor district. The Peshwa called her "Chhabili", which means "beautiful " and "lively and cheerful". She was educated at home and was taught to read and write, and was more independent in her childhood than others of her age; her studies included shooting, horsemanship, fencing and mallakhamba with her childhood friends Nana Sahib and Tantia Tope. Rani Lakshmibai contrasted many of the patriarchal cultural expectations for women in India's society at this time. And she was known for her unique perspectives and her courage to fight against social norms even in front of the whole society. Rani Lakshmibai was accustomed to riding on horseback accompanied by escorts between the palace and the temple, although sometimes she was carried in a palanquin. Her horses included Sarangi, Pavan and Baadal; according to historians, she rode Baadal when escaping from the fort in 1858. Her palace, the Rani Mahal, has now been converted into a museum. It houses a collection of archaeological remains of the period between the 9th and 12th centuries AD.*

## History of Jhansi, 1842 – May 1857

*Manikarnika was married to the Maharaja of Jhansi, Gangadhar Rao Newalkar, in May 1844 and was afterward called Lakshmibai in honor of the Hindu goddess Devi Lakshmi and according to the Maharashtrian tradition of women being given a new name after marriage. In September 1851, she gave birth to a boy, later named Damodar Rao, who died four months after birth due to a chronic illness. The Maharaja adopted a child called Anand Rao, the son of Gangadhar Rao's cousin, who was renamed Damodar Rao, on the day before the Maharaja died. The adoption was in the presence of the British political officer who was given a letter from the Maharaja instructing that the child be treated with respect and that the government of Jhansi should be given to his widow for her lifetime. After the death of the Maharaja in November 1853, because Damodar Rao (born Anand Rao) was an adopted son, the British East India Company, under Governor-General Lord Dalhousie, applied the Doctrine of Lapse, rejecting Damodar Rao's claim to the throne and annexing the state to its territories. When she was informed of this she cried out "Main apni Jhansi nahi doongi" (I shall not surrender my Jhansi). In March 1854, Rani Lakshmibai was given an annual pension of Rs. 60,000 and ordered to leave the palace and the fort. According to Vishnu Bhatt Godse, the Rani would exercise at weightlifting, wrestling, and steeplechasing before breakfast. An intelligent and simply-dressed woman, she ruled in a businesslike manner.*

## The Revolt of 1857

*On 10 May 1857, the Indian Rebellion started in Meerut. When news of the rebellion reached Jhansi, the Rani asked the British political officer, Captain Alexander Skene, for permission to raise a body of armed men for her protection; Skene agreed to this. The city was relatively calm amid the regional unrest in the summer of 1857, but the Rani conducted a Haldi Kumkum ceremony with pomp in front of all the women of Jhansi to provide assurance to her subjects, and to convince them that the British were cowards and not to be afraid of them. Until this point, Lakshmi Bai was reluctant to rebel against the British. In June 1857, rebels of the 12ᵗʰ Bengal Native Infantry seized the Star Fort of Jhansi, containing the treasure and magazine, and after persuading the British to lay down their arms by promising them no harm, broke their word and massacred 40 to 60 European officers of the garrison along with their wives and children. The Rani's involvement in this massacre is still a subject of debate. An army doctor, Thomas Lowe, wrote after the rebellion characterizing her as the "Jezebel of India ... the young rani upon whose head rested the blood of the slain".*

## The Rani of Jhansi's seal

*Four days after the massacre the sepoys left Jhansi, having obtained a large sum of money from the Rani, and having threatened to blow up the palace where she lived. Following this, as the only source of authority in the city the Rani felt obliged to assume the administration and wrote to Major Erskine, commissioner of the Saugor division explaining the events which had led her to do so. On 2 July, Erskine wrote in reply, requesting her to "manage the District for the British Government" until the arrival of a British Superintendent. The Rani's forces defeated an attempt by the mutineers to assert the claim to the throne of a rival prince Sadashiv Rao (nephew of Maharaja Gangadhar Rao) who was captured and imprisoned. There was then an invasion of Jhansi by the forces of Company allies Orchha and Datia; their intention however was to divide Jhansi between themselves. The Rani appealed to the British for aid but it was now believed by the governor-general that she was responsible for the massacre and no reply was received. She set up a foundry to cast cannon to be used on the walls of the fort and assembled forces including some from former feudatories of Jhansi and elements of the mutineers which were able to defeat the invaders in August 1857. Her intention at this time was still to hold Jhansi on behalf of the British.*

## Siege of Jhansi

*From August 1857 to January 1858, Jhansi under the Rani's rule was at peace. The British had announced that troops would be sent there to maintain control but the fact that none arrived strengthened the position of a party of her advisers who wanted independence from British rule. When the British forces finally arrived in March they found it well-defended and the fort had heavy guns which could fire over the town and nearby countryside. According to one source Hugh Rose, commanding the British forces, demanded the surrender of the city; if this was refused it would be destroyed. The same source claims that after due deliberation the Rani issued a proclamation: "We fight for independence. In the words of Lord Krishna, we will if we are victorious, enjoy the fruits of victory, if defeated and killed on the field of battle, we shall surely earn eternal glory and salvation." Other sources, for example, have no mention of a demand for surrender. She defended Jhansi against British troops when Sir Hugh Rose besieged Jhansi on 23 March 1858. The bombardment of Jhansi began on 24 March but was met by heavy return fire and the damaged defences were repaired. The defenders sent appeals for help to Tatya Tope, an important leader of the 1857 Indian Rebellion; an army of more than 20,000, headed by Tatya Tope, was sent to relieve Jhansi but they failed to do so when they fought the British on 31 March. During the battle with Tatya Tope's forces, part of the British forces continued the siege and by 2 April it was decided to launch an assault by a breach in the walls. Four columns assaulted the defences at different points and those attempting to scale the walls came under heavy fire. Two other columns had already entered the city and were approaching the palace together. Determined resistance was encountered in every street and every room of the palace. Street fighting continued into the following day and no quarter was given, even to women and children. "No maudlin clemency was to mark the fall of the city," wrote Thomas Lowe. The Rani withdrew from the palace to the fort and after taking counsel decided that since resistance in the city was useless she must leave and join either Tatya Tope or Rao Sahib (Nana Sahib's nephew). According to tradition, with Damodar Rao on her back she jumped on her horse Baadal from the fort; they survived but the horse died. The Rani escaped in the night with her son, surrounded by guards. The escort included the warriors Khuda Bakhsh Basharat Ali (commandant), Ghulam Gaus Khan, Dost Khan, Lala Bhau Bakshi, Moti Bai, Sunder-Mundar, Kashi Bai, Deewan Raghunath Singh and Deewan Jawahar Singh.[citation needed] She decamped to Kalpi with a few guards, where she joined additional rebel forces, including Tatya Tope. They occupied the town of Kalpi and prepared to defend it. On 22 May British forces attacked Kalpi; the forces were commanded by the Rani herself and were again defeated.*

## Flight to Gwalior

*The leaders (the Rani of Jhansi, Tatiya Tope, the Nawab of Banda, and Rao Sahib) fled once more. They came to Gwalior and joined the Indian forces who now held the city (Maharaja Scindia having fled to Agra from the battlefield at Morar). They moved on to Gwalior intending to occupy the strategic Gwalior Fort and the rebel forces occupied the city without opposition. The rebels proclaimed Nana Sahib as Peshwa of a revived Maratha dominion with Rao Sahib as his governor (ਸੂਬੇਦਾਰ) in Gwalior. The Rani was unsuccessful in trying to persuade the other rebel leaders to prepare to defend Gwalior against a British attack which she expected would come soon. General Rose's forces took Morar on 16 June and then made a successful attack on the city.*

## Death and aftermath

*On 17 June in Kotah-ki-Serai near the Phool Bagh of Gwalior, a squadron of the 8th (King's Royal Irish) Hussars, under Captain Heneage, fought the large Indian force commanded by Rani Lakshmibai, who was trying to leave the area. The 8th Hussars charged into the Indian force, slaughtering 5,000 Indian soldiers, including any Indian "over the age of 16". They took two guns and continued the charge right through the Phool Bagh encampment. In this engagement, according to an eyewitness account, Rani Lakshmibai put on a sowar's uniform and attacked one of the hussars; she was unhorsed and also wounded, probably by his saber. Shortly afterward, as she sat bleeding by the roadside, she recognized the soldier and fired at him with a pistol, whereupon he "dispatched the young lady with his carbine". According to another tradition Rani Lakshmibai, the Queen of Jhansi, dressed as a cavalry leader, was badly wounded; not wishing the British to capture her body, she told a hermit to burn it. After her death, a few local people cremated her body.*

# CHAPTER ELEVEN

# UDHAM SINGH

**Summary:**

*Udham Singh was an Indian revolutionary belonging to Ghadar Party and HSRA, best known for assassinating Michael O'Dwyer, the former lieutenant governor of the Punjab in India, on 13 March 1940. The assassination was done in revenge for the Jallianwala Bagh massacre in Amritsar in 1919, for which O'Dwyer was responsible and of which Singh himself was a survivor. Singh was subsequently tried and convicted of murder and hanged in July 1940. While in custody, he used the name 'Ram Mohammad Singh Azad', which represents the three major religions in India and his anti-colonial sentiment. Udham Singh was a well-known figure of the Indian independence movement. He is also referred to as Shaheed-i-Azam Sardar Udham Singh (the expression "Shaheed-i-Azam" means "the great martyr"). A district (Udham Singh Nagar) was named after him as a homage by the Mayawati government in October 1995.*

**UDHAM SINGH**

## Background

*Udham Singh was born 'Sher Singh' into a Sikh family on 26 December 1899 in the neighbourhood of Pilbad in Sunam, around 130 miles south of Lahore, British India, to Tehal Singh, a Kamboj, low-skilled low-paid manual labourer and his wife Narain Kaur. He was their youngest, with a two-year difference between him and his elder brother, Sadhu. When they were around age three and five respectively, their mother died. The two boys subsequently stayed close to their father while he worked in the village of Nilowal carrying mud from a newly constructed canal, part of Punjab Canal Colonies. After being laid off he found work as a railway crossing watchman in the village of Upali. In October 1907, whilst taking his sons by foot to Amritsar, their father collapsed and died at Ram Bagh Hospital. The two brothers were subsequently handed to an uncle who being unable to keep them, gave them to the Central Khalsa Orphanage, where according to the orphanage register, they were initiated on 28 October. Rebaptised, Sadhu became "Mukta", meaning "one who has escaped re-incarnation", and Sher Singh was renamed "Udham Singh", Udham meaning "the upheaval". At the orphanage he was affectionately referred to as "Ude". In 1917, Mukta died of an unknown sudden illness. Shortly thereafter, despite being below the official age of enrolment, Udham Singh persuaded authorities to allow him to serve in the British Indian Army during the First World War. He was subsequently attached to the lowest ranking labour unit with the 32ⁿᵈ Sikh Pioneers to work on restoration on the field railway from the coast up to Basra.[8] His young age and conflicts with authority led him to return to Punjab in less than six months. In 1918, he rejoined the army and was despatched to Basra and then Baghdad, where he carried out carpentry and general maintenance of machinery and vehicles, returning after a year to the orphanage in Amritsar in early 1919.*

## Massacre at Jallianwala Bagh

*On 10 April 1919, a number of local leaders allied to the Indian National Congress, including Satyapal and Saifuddin Kitchlew, were arrested under the terms of the Rowlatt Act. A military picket fired on a protesting crowd, precipitating a riot which saw numerous European-owned banks attacked and several Europeans attacked in the streets. On 13 April, over twenty thousand unarmed people were assembled in Jallianwala Bagh, Amritsar to celebrate the important Sikh festival of Baisakhi, and to peacefully protest the arrests. Singh and his friends from the orphanage were serving water to the crowd. Troops under the command of Colonel Reginald Dyer opened fire on the crowd, killing several hundred; this became known variously as the Amritsar Massacre or the Jallianwala Bagh massacre. Singh became involved in revolutionary politics and was deeply influenced by Bhagat Singh and his revolutionary group. In 1924, Singh became involved with the Ghadar Party, organising Indians overseas towards overthrowing colonial rule. In 1927, he returned to India on orders from Bhagat Singh, bringing 25 associates as well as revolvers and ammunition. Soon after, he was arrested for possession of unlicensed arms. Revolvers, ammunition, and copies of a prohibited Ghadar Party paper called "Ghadr-di-Gunj" ("Voice of Revolt") were confiscated. He was prosecuted and sentenced to five years in prison. Upon his release from prison in 1931, Singh's movements were under constant surveillance by the Punjab Police. He made his way to Kashmir, where he was able to evade the police and escape to Germany. In 1934, he reached London, where he found employment. Privately, he formed plans to assassinate Michael O'Dwyer. In Singh's diaries for 1939 and 1940, he occasionally misspells*

*O'Dwyer's surname as "O'Dyer", leaving a possibility he may have confused O'Dwyer with General Dyer. However, General Dyer had died in 1927, even before Udham Singh had planned the revenge. In England, Singh was affiliated to the Indian Workers' Association in Coventry and attended their meetings.*

## Shooting at Caxton Hall

*On 13 March 1940, Michael O'Dwyer was scheduled to speak at a joint meeting of the East India Association and the Central Asian Society (now Royal Society for Asian Affairs) at Caxton Hall, London. Singh had entered the event with a ticket in his wife's name. Singh concealed a revolver inside a book, which had pages cut in the shape of a revolver. This revolver was purchased by him from a soldier in a pub. Then he entered the hall and found an empty seat. As the meeting concluded, Singh shot O'Dwyer twice as he moved towards the speaking platform. One of these bullets passed through O'Dwyer's heart and right lung, killing him almost instantly. Others injured in the shooting included Sir Louis Dane; Lawrence Dundas, 2nd Marquess of Zetland and Charles Cochrane-Baillie, 2nd Baron Lamington. Singh was arrested immediately after the shooting and the pistol (now in the Crime Museum) seized as evidence.*

## Personal life

*Udham Singh married a Mexican woman in the 1920s, by whom he fathered two sons. Udham Singh's wife was named Lupe Hernandez. In 1927 he left the United States, leaving Lupe and their two sons behind. Many other Indian men in the States took Hispanic wives due to the Johnson-Reed (Immigration) Act of 1924, as they would otherwise have been expelled. According to some of his relatives, Udham Singh later took an English wife as well. It is not known if he had children with her too.*

## Murder, trial, and execution

*On 1 April 1940, Singh was formally charged with the murder of Michael O'Dwyer, and remanded in custody at Brixton Prison. Initially asked to explain his motivations, Singh stated:*

*"I did it because I had a grudge against him. He deserved it. I don't belong to society or anything else. I don't care. I don't mind dying. What is the use of waiting until you get old? ... Is Zetland dead? He ought to be. I put two into him. I bought the revolver from a soldier in a public house. My parents died when I was three or four. Only one dead? I thought I could get more."*

*While in custody, he called himself Ram Mohammad Singh Azad: the first three words of the name reflect the three major religious communities of Punjab (Hindu, Muslim, and Sikh); the last word azad (literally "free") reflects his anti-colonial sentiment. While awaiting his trial, Singh went on a 42-day hunger strike, before finally being force fed. On 4 June 1940, his trial commenced at the Central Criminal Court, Old Bailey, before Justice Cyril Atkinson, with V.K. Krishna Menon and St John Hutchinson representing him. G. B. McClure was the prosecuting barrister. When asked about his motivation, Singh explained:*

*I did it because I had a grudge against him. He deserved it. He was the real culprit. He wanted to crush the spirit of my people, so I have crushed him. For full 21 years, I have been trying to seek vengeance. I am happy that I have done the job. I am not scared of death. I am dying for my country. I have seen my people starving in India under the British rule. I have protested against this, it was my duty.*

*Singh was convicted of murder and sentenced to death. On 31 July 1940, Singh was hanged at Pentonville Prison by Albert Pierrepoint. His remains are preserved at the Jallianwala Bagh in Amritsar, Punjab. On every 31 July, marches are held in Sunam (Singh's hometown) by various organisations and every statue of Singh in the city is paid tribute with flower garlands.*

# LALA LAJPAT RAI


**Summary:**

*Lala Lajpat Rai was an Indian revolutionary, politician, and author, popularly known as Punjab Kesari. He was one of the three members of the Lal Bal Pal trio. He died of severe head trauma injuries sustained 18 days earlier during a baton charge by police in Lahore, when he led a peaceful protest march against the British Simon Commission Indian constitutional reforms.*

**LALA LAJPAT RAI**

## Background

*Lajpat Rai was born on 28 January 1865 into an Agrawal Jain family as the eldest son of six children of Munshi Radha Krishna, an Urdu and Persian government school teacher and Gulab Devi Aggarwal at Dhudike in the Faridkot district of the Punjab Province of British India (now in Moga district, Punjab, India). He spent much of his youth in Jagraon. His house still stands in Jagraon and houses a library and museum. He also built the first educational institute R.K. High school in Jagraon.*

## Education

*Lajpat Rai had his initial education in Government Higher Secondary School, Rewari, Punjab province, where his father was posted as an Urdu teacher. In 1880, he joined Government College at Lahore to study law, where he came in contact with patriots and future freedom fighters, such as Lala Hans Raj and Pandit Guru Dutt. While studying at Lahore he was influenced by the Hindu reformist movement of Swami Dayanand Saraswati, became a member of the existing Arya Samaj Lahore (founded 1877) and founder-editor of Lahore-based Arya Gazette.*

## Career

## *Law*

*In 1884, his father was transferred to Rohtak, and Rai came along after the completion of his studies at Lahore. In 1886, he moved to Hisar where his father was transferred, and started to practice law and became a founding member of the Bar Council of Hisar along with Babu Churamani. In the same year, he helped Mahatma Hansraj establish the nationalistic Dayananda Anglo-Vedic School, Lahore, and he also founded the Hisar district branches of the Indian National Congress, and the reformist Arya Samaj movement with several other local leaders. These included Babu Churamani (lawyer), the three Tayal brothers (Chandu Lal Tayal, Hari Lal Tayal and Balmokand Tayal), Dr. Ramji Lal Hooda, Dr. Dhani Ram, Arya Samaj Pandit Murari Lal, Seth Chhaju Ram Jat (founder of Jat School, Hisar) and Dev Raj Sandhir. In 1888 and again in 1889, he had the honour of being one of the four delegates from Hisar to attend the annual session of the Congress at Allahabad, along with Babu Churamani, Lala Chhabil Das and Seth Gauri Shankar. In 1892, he moved to Lahore to practise before the Lahore High Court. To shape the political policy of India to gain independence, he also practised journalism, and was a regular contributor to several newspapers including The Tribune. He was also associated with the management of Punjab National Bank and Lakshmi Insurance Company in their early stages in 1894. In 1914, he quit law practise to dedicate himself to the Indian independence movement and travelled to Britain, and then to the United States in 1917. In*

*October 1917, he founded the Indian Home Rule League of America in New York. He stayed in the United States from 1917 to 1920. His early freedom struggle was impacted by Arya Samaj and communal representation.*

## Politics

*After joining the Indian National Congress and taking part in political agitation in Punjab, Lala Lajpat Rai Wadwal was deported to Mandalay, but there was insufficient evidence to hold him for subversion. Lajpat Rai's supporters attempted to secure his election to the presidency of the party session at Surat in December 1907, but he did not succeed. Graduates of the National College, which he founded inside the Bradlaugh Hall at Lahore as an alternative to British-style institutions, included Bhagat Singh. He was elected President of the Indian National Congress in the Calcutta Special Session of 1920. In 1921, he founded Servants of the People Society, a non-profit welfare organisation, in Lahore, which shifted its base to Delhi after partition, and has branches in many parts of India. According to him, Hindu society needs to fight its own battle with caste system, position of women and untouchability. Vedas were an important part of Hindu religion and approved everyone should be allowed to read them and recite the mantras. He believed that everyone should be allowed to read and learn from the Vedas.*

## Travel to the United States

*Lajpat Rai travelled to the United States in 1916, and then returned during World War I. He toured Sikh communities along the Western Seaboard, visited the Tuskegee University in Alabama, and met with workers in the Philippines. His travelogue, The United States of America (1916), details these travels and features extensive quotations from leading African American intellectuals, including W.E.B. Du Bois and Booker T. Washington. While in the United States he had founded the Indian Home Rule League in New York City and a monthly journal, the Young India and Hindustan Information Services Association. Rai petitioned the United States House Committee on Foreign Affairs, painting a vivid picture of maladministration by the British Raj in India, the aspirations of Indian public for independence amongst many other points which strongly sought the support of the international community for the attainment of Indian independence. The 32-page petition, which was prepared overnight, was discussed in the U.S. Senate in October 1917. The book also argues for the notion of "color-caste," suggesting sociological similarities between race in the US and caste in India. During World War I, Lajpat Rai lived in the United States, but he returned to India in 1919 and in the following year led the special session of the Indian National Congress that launched the non-co-operation movement. He was imprisoned from 1921 to 1923 and elected to the legislative assembly on his release.*

## Protests Against The Simon Commission

*In 1928, the United Kingdom set up the Simon Commission, headed by Sir John Simon to report on the political situation in India. The commission was boycotted by Indian political parties because it did not include any Indian members, and it was met with country-wide protests. When the Commission visited Lahore on 30 October 1928, Lajpat Rai led a non-violent march in protest against it and gave the slogan "Simon Go Back!". The protesters chanted the slogan and carried black flags. The police superintendent in Lahore, James A. Scott, ordered the police to lathi charge the protesters and personally assaulted Rai. Despite being severely injured, Rai subsequently addressed the crowd and said "I declare that the blows struck at me today will be the last nails in the coffin of British rule in India."*

## Death

*Rai did not fully recover from his injuries and died on 17 November 1928. Doctors thought that James Scott's blows had hastened his death. However, when the matter was raised in the British Parliament, the British government denied any role in Rai's death. Bhagat Singh, an HSRA revolutionary who was a witness to the event, swore to avenge the death of Rai, who was a significant leader of the Indian independence movement. He joined other revolutionaries, Shivaram Rajguru, Sukhdev Thapar and Chandra Shekhar Azad, in a plot to kill Scott to send a message to the British government. However, in a case of mistaken identity, Singh was signalled to shoot on the appearance of John P. Saunders, an assistant superintendent of the Lahore Police. He was shot by Rajguru and Singh while leaving the District Police Headquarters in Lahore on 17 December 1928. Chanan Singh, a head constable who was chasing them, was fatally injured by Azad's covering fire. This case did not stop Singh and his fellow-members of the Hindustan Socialist Republican Association from claiming that retribution had been exacted.*

# MADAN MOHAN MALVIYA

**Summary:**

*Madan Mohan Malaviya was an Indian scholar, educational reformer and politician notable for his role in the Indian independence movement. He was president of the Indian National Congress three times and the founder of Akhil Bharat Hindu Mahasabha. He was addressed as Pandit, a title of respect.*

## PANDIT MADAN MOHAN MALVIYA

## Life and education

*Malaviya was born in Prayagraj, India on 25 December 1861, into a Gaur Brahmin family to Brijnath Malaviya and Moona Devi. He was born in a locality known as Lal Diggi (Malviya Nagar) in a small house of Sawal Das of Saryakund. His grandfather, Premdhar Prasad, was the son of Vishnu Prasad. Since they hailed from Malwa (Ujjain) in the present-day state of Madhya Pradesh, they came to be known as 'Malaviya'. Of his ardent love for the Malwa region, where his family belonged, he adopted the surname "Malaviya" instead of Chaturvedi. He married Kundan Devi from Mirzapur at sixteen. His ancestors were highly respected for their learning and knowledge of Hindu scriptures and Sanskrit scholarship. His father also learned in Sanskrit scriptures and used to recite the Srimad Bhagavatam. Malaviya's education began at the age of five in Mahajani Pathsala. Later, he joined Hardeva's Dharma Gyanopadesh Pathshala, completed his primary education and joined a school run by Vidha Vardini Sabha. He then joined Allahabad Zila School (Allahabad District School), where he started writing poems under the pen name Makarand which were published in journals and magazines. Malaviya matriculated in 1879 from the Muir Central College, now known as the University of Allahabad. Harrison College's Principal provided a monthly scholarship to Malaviya, whose family had been facing financial hardships, and he was able to complete his B.A. at the University of Calcutta. Malaviya desired to pursue an M.A. in Sanskrit. Still, family circumstances did not allow him to do so, and his father wanted him to pursue the family profession of Bhagavat recital instead. In July 1884, Madan Mohan Malaviya began his professional career as an assistant master at the Government High School in Allahabad.*

## Politics

*Malaviya started his political career in 1886 with an address to the Indian National Congress session in Calcutta. Malaviya would go on to become one of the most powerful political leaders of his time, being elected Congress president on four occasions. In December 1886, Malaviya attended the second Indian National Congress session in Calcutta under the chairmanship of Dadabhai Naoroji, where he spoke on the issue of representation in Councils. His address not only impressed Dadabhai but also Raja Rampal Singh, ruler of Kalakankar estate near Allahabad, who had founded a Hindi weekly, Hindustan, but was still looking for a suitable editor to turn it into a daily. In July 1887, Malaviya resigned from the school and joined as editor of the nationalist weekly. He remained for two and a half years, and left for Allahabad to study for his L.L.B.. In Allahabad, he was offered the co-editorship of The Indian Opinion, an English daily. After finishing his law degree, he started practicing law at Allahabad District Court in 1891, and moved to Allahabad High Court by December 1893. Malaviya became the President of the Indian National Congress in 1909, a position he held also in 1918. He was a moderate leader and opposed separate electorates for Muslims under the Lucknow Pact of 1916. The "Mahamana" title was conferred on him by Mahatma Gandhi. Malaviya renounced his practice of law in 1911 to fulfil his resolve to serve the causes of education and social service. Despite this vow, on one occasion when 177 freedom fighters were convicted to be hanged in the Chauri-chaura case, he appeared before the court and won the acquittal of 156 freedom fighters. He followed the tradition of Sannyas throughout his life, adhering to his avowed commitment to live on the support of society. He was a member of the Imperial Legislative Council from 1912 until 1919, when it was converted to the Central Legislative Assembly, of which he remained a member until 1926. Malaviya was an important figure in the Non-cooperation movement. He was opposed to the politics of appeasement and the participation of Congress in the Khilafat movement. In 1928, he joined Lala Lajpat Rai, Jawaharlal Nehru, and many others in protesting against the Simon Commission, which had been set up by the British to consider India's future. Just as the "Buy British" campaign was sweeping England, he issued a manifesto on 30 May 1932 urging concentration on the "Buy Indian" movement in India. Malaviya was a delegate at the Second Round Table Conference in 1931. During the Salt March, he was arrested on 25 April 1932 along with 450 other Congress volunteers in Delhi, only a few days after he was appointed as the President of Congress following the arrest of Sarojini Naidu. In 1933, at Calcutta, Malaviya was again appointed as the President of the Congress. Before Independence, Malaviya was the only leader of the Indian National Congress to be appointed as its president for four terms. On 24 September 1932, an agreement known as Poona Pact was signed between Dr. B R Ambedkar (on behalf of the depressed classes among Hindus) and Mahatma Gandhi (on behalf of the other Hindus). The agreement guaranteed reserved seats for the depressed classes in the Provisional legislatures within the general electorate, and not by creating a separate electorate. Due to the pact, the depressed class received 148 seats in the legislature, instead of the 71 as allocated in the Communal Award proposal of the British Prime Minister Ramsay MacDonald. After the pact, the Communal Award was modified to include the terms as per the pacts. The text uses the term "Depressed Classes" to denote Untouchables among Hindus who were later called Scheduled Castes and Scheduled Tribes under India Act 1935, and in the Indian Constitution of 1950. In protest against the Communal Award to provide separate electorates for minorities, Malaviya and Madhav Shrihari Aney left the Congress and started the Congress Nationalist Party. The party contested the 1934 elections to the central legislature and won 12 seats.*

## Journalistic career

*Malaviya started his journalistic career as Editor of the Hindi daily Hindostan in 1887. Raja Rampal Singh of Kalakankar (Pratapgadh District), impressed by the speech and personality of Malaviya during the second Congress Session in Calcutta held in 1886, requested him to assume this position. In 1889, he became the Editor of the "Indian Opinion". After the incorporation of "Indian Opinion" with the "Advocate" of Lucknow, Malaviya started his own Hindi weekly "Abhyudaya"(1907–1909 under his editorship). Malaviya's poems (sawaiyas) were published sometime in 1883–84 under the pseudonym of 'Makrand' in 'Harischandra Chandrika' magazine (published by Bharatendu Harishchandra). His articles on religious and contemporary subjects were published in 'Hindi Pradeepa'. When the British government promulgated The Newspaper (Incitement to Offences) Act in 1908 and the Indian Press Act, 1910, Malaviya started a campaign against them and called for an All India Conference in Allahabad. He then realized the need of an English newspaper to make the campaign effective throughout the country. As a result, with the help of Motilal Nehru, he started an English daily the "Leader" in 1909, where he was Editor (1909–1911) and President (1911–1919). In 1924, Malaviya along with the help of national leaders Lala Lajpat Rai, M. R. Jayakar and industrialist Ghanshyam Das Birla, acquired The Hindustan Times and saved it from an untimely demise. Malaviya raised Rs. 50,000 for the acquisition, with Birla paying most of it. Malaviya was the Chairman of Hindustan Times from 1924 to 1946. His efforts resulted in the launch of its Hindi edition 'Hindustan' in 1936. The paper is now owned by the Birla family. In 1933, Malaviya started Sanatana Dharma from BHU, a magazine dedicated to religious, dharmic interests.*

**Legal career**

*In 1891, Malaviya completed his LL.B. from Allahabad University and started practice in Allahabad District Court. He practised at the High*

*Court from 1893. He earned significant respect as one of the most brilliant lawyers of the Allahabad High Court. He gave up his legal practice when at his pinnacle in 1911 on his 50th birthday so that he could serve the nation thereafter. About his legal career, Sir Tej Bahadur Sapru regarded him ...a brilliant Civil Lawyer and Sir Mirza Ismail said – I have heard a great lawyer say that if Mr. Malaviya had so willed it, he would have been an ornament to the legal profession. Malaviya only donned his lawyer's robe once more, in 1924 following the Chauri Chaura incident in which a police station was attacked and set on fire in February 1922, as a result of which Mahatma Gandhi called off the then launched Non-cooperation movement. The sessions court had sentenced 170 persons to the gallows for the attack. However, Malaviya defended them in the Allahabad High Court and was able to save 155 of them. The remaining 15 also were recommended for clemency by the High Court, whereafter their sentences were commuted from death to life imprisonment.*

## Banaras Hindu University

*In April 1911, Annie Besant met Malaviya and they decided to work for a common Hindu University in Varanasi. Besant and fellow trustees of the Central Hindu College, which she had founded in 1898, also agreed to the Government of India's precondition that the college become a part of the new university. Thus Banaras Hindu University (BHU) was established in 1916, through a Parliamentary legislation, the 'Banaras Hindu University Act of 1915', and today it remains a prominent institution of learning in India. In 1939, he left the Vice-Chancellorship of BHU and was succeeded by S. Radhakrishnan, who later became the President of India. Spread over 16.5 km2 (4,100 acres) with a student population of about 30,000, BHU is the largest residential university in Asia. Malaviya' son Pandit Govind Malaviya served as the Vice-Chancellor of BHU from 1948 to 1951. His grandson Justice Giridhar Malaviya is currently the Chancellor of BHU since 2018.*

## Social service

*Malaviya founded Ganga Mahasabha to oppose the damming of the Ganga. He compelled the British government to sign an agreement with Ganga Mahasabha and other Hindu religious leaders on uninterrupted flow of the Ganga in Haridwar and protection from any future obstruction. This agreement is known as Aviral Ganga Raksha Samjhuata 1916 or the Agreement of 1916. Malaviya played an important part in the removal of untouchability and in giving direction to the Harijan movement. The Harijan Sevak Sangh was founded at a meeting in 1933 at which Pandit Malaviya presided. Malaviya asserted – if you admit internal purity of human soul, you or your religion can never get impure or defiled in any way by touch or association with any man. To solve the problem of untouchability, Malaviya followed a Hindu method, of giving Mantradīkshā to untouchables. He said, "Mantras would be a certain means of their upliftment socially, politically and spiritually." He worked for the eradication of caste barriers in temples and other social barriers. Malaviya contributed significantly to ensuring the entry of the so-called untouchables into any Hindu temple. In March 1936, Hindu Dalit (Harijan) leader P. N. Rajbhoj along with a group of 200 Dalit people demanded entry at the Kalaram Temple on a Rath Yatra day. Malaviya in the presence of priests of Kalaram Temple, gave diksha to the assembled people and facilitated their entry into the temple. They then also participated in the Rath Yatra of Kalaram Temple. He established Bharati Bhawan Library on 15 December 1889 with his friend Lala Brajmohan Jee Bhalla in Allahabad. In 1901 Malaviya established a boys' hostel named Hindu Hostel (Hindu Boarding House) in Allahabad.*

## Scouting

*Scouting in India was initially introduced by Robert Baden Powell, though only British, European and Anglo Indian students could join the organization known as British Boy Scouts. Scouting for native Indians was started by Justice Vivian Bose, after independence in 1947. Officials from Hindustan Scouts and Guides were hired by the Government of India when the country became independent to continue the functioning of British Boy Scouts, renamed as The Bharat Scouts and Guides. Newspaper reports of the resignation of Indian Railways Officer Sri Ram Vajpei on grounds of racial discrimination despite being qualified in scouting with its highest degree LT, in England prompted the then President of Congress Malaviya to inform himself about the scouting movement. With the support of other members, Hridayanath Kunzru, Girija Shankar Bajpai, Annie Besant and George Arundale, Malaviya started an organisation called the All India Seva Samiti under Sewa Bharti unit to conduct scouting activities. While the British refused initially to recognize the scouting education imparted by the Samiti, Baden Powell himself advocated the recognition of Indian Scouting as co-curricular education in school, after a visit to India afforded him the opportunity to learn of the association's activities.*